T4-APV-752

MOSAIC I
A Content-Based Writing Book

Laurie Blass **Meredith Pike-Baky**
University of California, Berkeley

RANDOM HOUSE **NEW YORK**

This book was developed for Random House by Eirik Børve, Inc.

First Edition

9 8 7 6 5 4 3 2

Copyright © 1985 by Random House, Inc.

All rights reserved under International and Pan-American Copyright Conventions. No part of this book may be reproduced in any form or by any means, electronic or mechanical, including photocopying, without permission in writing from the publisher. All inquiries should be addressed to Random House, Inc., 201 East 50th Street, New York, N.Y. 10022. Published in the United States by Random House, Inc., and simultaneously in Canada by Random House of Canada Limited, Toronto.

Library of Congress Cataloging in Publication Data

Blass, Laurie, 1952–
 Mosaic I, a content-based writing book.

 "Developed for Random House by Eirik Børve, Inc."
 Includes index.
 1. English language—Text-books for foreign speakers.
2. English language—Rhetoric. I. Pike-Baky, Meredith,
1948– . II. Eirik Børve, Inc. III. Title. IV. Title:
Mosaic one, a content-based writing book.
PE1128.B5925   1985   808'.042   85–1810
ISBN 0–394–33715–8 (pbk.)

Manufactured in the United States of America

Text design by Janet Bollow
Cover design by Cheryl Carrington
Cover photograph: Peter Menzel
Technical art: Brenda Booth
Cartoons: Jim M'Guinness
Photo Research: Stuart Kenter
Composition by Dharma Press
ISBN: 394–33715–8

ACKNOWLEDGMENTS

155 "Why a Liberal Arts Major Makes Business Sense," *Glamour*, February 1984. Courtesy *Glamour*. Copyright © 1984 by The Condé Nast Publications. Inc. **178** Adapted by permission of the author and publishers from *Never in Anger: Portrait of an Eskimo Family* by Jean L. Briggs, Cambridge, Mass.: Harvard University Press, Copyright © 1970 by the President and Fellows of Harvard College. **199** "Nonverbal Behavior" by Fathi S. Yousef. From *Intercultural Communication: A Reader*, Second Edition, by Larry A. Samovar and Richard E. Porter. © 1976 by Wadsworth Publishing Company, Inc. Reprinted by permission of Wadsworth Publishing Company, Belmont, California 94002, and Fathi S. Yousef. **222** "U.S. Passports Changing with Technology" by James E. Roper. Reprinted by permission of Newhouse News Service. **243** "What is Intelligence, Anyway?" by Isaac Asimov. Reprinted by permission of the author.

PHOTO CREDITS

1 Hugh Rogers, Monkmeyer. **2** Mike Mazzaschi, Stock, Boston. **3** (top) Owen Franken, Stock, Boston; (bottom) Peter Menzel. **4** (top) Charles Gatewood, Stock, Boston; (middle) John R. Maher, EKM-Nepenthe; (bottom) © George E. Jones, Photo Researchers. **29** © Peter G. Aitken, Photo Researchers. **30** (top left) Owen Franken, Stock, Boston; (top right) Arthur Grace, Stock, Boston; (bottom left) © Ellan Young, Photo Researchers; (bottom right) Russell Abraham, Stock, Boston. **51** Patrick Ward, Stock, Boston. **52** (top) © Christa Armstrong, Photo Researchers; (middle) James R. Holland, Stock, Boston; (bottom left) James R. Holland, Stock, Boston; (bottom right) Joan Liften, Archive. **69** © Bohdan Heynewych, Stock, Boston. **70** (top left) Owen Franken, Stock, Boston; (middle right) Ellis Herwig, Stock, Boston; (bottom left) © David R. Frazier, Photo Researchers; (bottom right) Cary Wolinsky, Stock, Boston. **89** James R. Holland, Stock, Boston. **91** © San Francisco Examiner. **109** © Fritz Henle, Photo Researchers. **110** (top) Ellis Herwig, Stock, Boston; (bottom left) © George W. Gardner, Stock, Boston; (bottom right) George Bellerose, Stock, Boston. **111** (top) Christopher Brown, Stock, Boston; (middle) Owen Franken, Stock, Boston; (bottom) Peter Menzel. **129** James R. Holland, Stock, Boston. **130** (top) UPI/Bettmann; (bottom) © Louis Goldman, Photo Researchers. **131** (top left) R. Capa, Magnum; (top center) © Standford H. Roth, Photo Researchers; (top right) © Richard Frieman, Photo Researchers; (bottom) UPI/Bettmann. **132** (top) UPI/Bettmann; (bottom) © Patrice Flesch, Stock, Boston. **149** © Chris Perkins, Magnum. **150** (top) Cary Wolinsky, Stock, Boston; (bottom left) © Fredrik D. Bodin, Stock, Boston; (bottom right) © Nancy J. Pierce, Photo Researchers. **151** (top left) Peter Menzel; (top right) Robert George Gaylord, EKM-Nepenthe; (bottom left) © Judy S. Gelles, Stock, Boston; (bottom right) Bohdan Heynewych, Stock, Boston. **173** Peter Southwick, Stock, Boston. **174** (top left) Ira Kirschenbaum, Stock, Boston; (top right) Courtesy of the United Nations; (middle left) © Doiseau, Photo Researchers; (middle right) © Fritz Henle, Photo Researchers; (bottom left) Ira Kirschenbaum, Stock, Boston; (bottom right) © Victor Erslebert, Photo Researchers. **195** © Chester Higgins, Jr., Photo Researchers. **196** (top left) © John Maher, EKM-Nepenthe; (top right) © Lou Dematteis, Jeroboam; (middle left) © Bernard Pierre Wolff, Photo Researchers; (middle right) © Georg Gerster, Photo Researchers; (bottom left) Peter Menzel, Stock, Boston; (bottom right) Elizabeth Hamlin, Stock, Boston. **219** Peter Menzel. **220** (top left) © Tom McHugh, Photo Researchers; (top right) Peter Menzel; (middle left) Jean-Claude Lejeune, Stock, Boston; (middle right) NASA photo; (bottom left) Ellis Herwig, Stock, Boston; (bottom right) © Frank Siteman, EKM-Nepenthe. **237** ©Arthur Grace, Stock, Boston.

CONTENTS

Preface   xv

CHAPTER 1
NEW CHALLENGES   1

PART ONE: IDEAS FOR WRITING   2
Impressions of a New Culture   2
   Brainstorming   5
   Freewriting   5
   Reading for Ideas: "Adjusting to a New Culture"   6
   Gathering Information   8
PART TWO: LANGUAGE FOR WRITING   8
Describing Impressions of People, Places, and Things   9
Describing Problems   9
Asking Information Questions   10
   Practicing What You've Learned   12
PART THREE: SYSTEMS FOR WRITING   12
The Paragraph   12
The Topic Sentence   13
   Practicing What You've Learned   15
   Getting Started   23
   Assignments   24
PART FOUR: EVALUATING FOR REWRITING   26

CHAPTER 2

ACADEMIC LIFE 29

PART ONE: IDEAS FOR WRITING 31
Issues in Education 31
    Brainstorming 33
    Freewriting 34
    Reading for Ideas: "Losing Sight of Students,"
        by Thomas Patrick Melady 34
    Gathering Information 37
PART TWO: LANGUAGE FOR WRITING 38
Stating Advantages and Disadvantages 38
    Practicing What You've Learned 38
PART THREE: SYSTEMS FOR WRITING 39
Paragraph Unity 39
    Practicing What You've Learned 40
    Paragraph Organization: *TBER* 42
    Practicing What You've Learned 44
    Assignments 49
PART FOUR: EVALUATING FOR REWRITING 49

CHAPTER 3

THE FAMILY 51

PART ONE: IDEAS FOR WRITING 53
The Family in Transition 53
    Brainstorming 53
    Freewriting 54
    Reading for Ideas: "An Interview with Alice" 54
    Gathering Information 56
PART TWO: LANGUAGE FOR WRITING 57
Describing Roles, Relationships, and Feelings 57
    Practicing What You've Learned 58
PART THREE: SYSTEMS FOR WRITING 59
Paragraph Coherence: Pronouns and Paraphrasing 59
    Practicing What You've Learned 60
Paragraph Coherence:
    Transition Words and Expressions 61
    Practicing What You're Learning 62
    Assignments 66
PART FOUR: EVALUATING FOR REWRITING 66

CHAPTER 4

HEALTH
69

PART ONE: IDEAS FOR WRITING 71
Health and Everyday Living 71
  Brainstorming 71
  Freewriting 72
  Reading for Ideas: "Type A Behavior and Type B Solutions,"
    by Sam Keen and Tom Ferguson 73
  Gathering Information 76
PART TWO: LANGUAGE FOR WRITING 77
Showing Causes and Effects 77
  Practicing What You've Learned 78
Expressing Possibility and Probability 78
  Practicing What You've Learned 79
PART THREE: SYSTEMS FOR WRITING 81
Paragraph Development 81
  Types of Supporting Material 81
  Deepening the Discussion 82
  Practicing What You've Learned 84
Paragraph Organization 84
  Assignments 86
PART FOUR: EVALUATING FOR REWRITING 86

CHAPTER 5

MONEY MATTERS
89

PART ONE: IDEAS FOR WRITING 90
The Successful Entrepreneur 90
  Brainstorming 92
  Freewriting 93
  Reading for Ideas: "An Off-the Wall Success Story:
    Porter Hurt's Amazing Rise from Sheetrocker to
    High-Tech Millionaire," by John Eckhouse 93
  Gathering Information 97
PART TWO: LANGUAGE FOR WRITING 98
Describing Successful People 98
  Practicing What You've Learned 99
Turning Adjectives into Abstract Nouns 99
  Practicing What You've Learned 100

PART THREE: SYSTEMS FOR WRITING 101
Unity and Coherence Through Key Words and Concepts 101
    Practicing What You've Learned 103
    Assignments 105
PART FOUR: EVALUATING FOR REWRITING 106

CHAPTER 6

LEISURE TIME
109

PART ONE: IDEAS FOR WRITING 110
Leisure-Time Activities 110
    Brainstorming 112
    Freewriting 114
    Reading for Ideas: "The Olympic Games" 114
    Gathering Information 117
PART TWO: LANGUAGE FOR WRITING 118
Classifying Leisure-Time Activities 118
    Practicing What You've Learned 118
PART THREE: SYSTEMS FOR WRITING 119
Paragraph Development:
    General to Specific Information 119
    Practicing What You've Learned 124
    Assignments 125
PART FOUR: EVALUATING FOR REWRITING 125

CHAPTER 7

CREATIVITY
129

PART ONE: IDEAS FOR WRITING 130
Artists at Work 130
    Brainstorming 133
    Freewriting 134
    Reading for Ideas: "A Moveable Feast,"
        by Ernest Hemingway 134
    Gathering Information 137
PART TWO: LANGUAGE FOR WRITING 138
Making Comparisons 138
    Practicing What You've Learned 139

PART THREE: SYSTEMS FOR WRITING   140
Review of Paragraph Development and Organization   140
   Practicing What You've Learned   142
Organizing a Comparison Paragraph   143
   Practicing What You've Learned   144
   Assignments   145
PART FOUR: EVALUATING FOR REWRITING   146

CHAPTER 8

CHOICES   149

PART ONE: IDEAS FOR WRITING   150
Controversial Issues   150
   Brainstorming   152
   Freewriting   153
   Reading for Ideas: "Why a Liberal Arts Major
     Makes Business Sense," by Grace Hechinger   154
   Gathering Information   156
PART TWO: LANGUAGE FOR WRITING   159
Expressing a Point of View   159
   Practicing What You've Learned   159
Exposing the Other Side: Predicting the Outcome   160
   Practicing What You've Learned   161
PART THREE: SYSTEMS FOR WRITING   163
From Paragraph to Essay: The Expository Essay   163
   Practicing What You've Learned   167
   Assignments   169
PART FOUR: EVALUATING FOR REWRITING   170

CHAPTER 9

THE PHYSICAL WORLD   173

PART ONE: IDEAS FOR WRITING   175
Environment and Culture   175
   Brainstorming   176
   Freewriting   177
   Reading for Ideas: "Never in Anger:
     Portrait of an Eskimo Family," by Jean L. Briggs   178
   Gathering Information   181

PART TWO: LANGUAGE FOR WRITING   183
Describing Environmental Conditions   183
   Practicing What You've Learned   184
PART THREE: SYSTEMS FOR WRITING   185
The Thesis Statement   185
   Practicing What You've Learned   187
   Assignments   190
PART FOUR: EVALUATING FOR REWRITING   191

CHAPTER 10

HUMAN BEHAVIOR   195

PART ONE: IDEAS FOR WRITING   197
Nonverbal Behavior   197
   Brainstorming   197
   Freewriting   198
   Reading for Ideas: "Nonverbal Communication:
     Some Intricate and Diverse Dimensions in
     Intercultural Communication," by Fathi Yousef   199
   Gathering Information   205
PART TWO: LANGUAGE FOR WRITING   207
Interpreting Nonverbal Behavior   207
   Practicing What You've Learned   209
PART THREE: SYSTEMS FOR WRITING   209
Essay Organization   209
   Practicing What You've Learned   211
   Assignments   214
PART FOUR: EVALUATING FOR REWRITING   215

CHAPTER 11

TECHNOLOGY   219

PART ONE: IDEAS FOR WRITING   221
Technological Innovations   221
   Brainstorming   221
   Freewriting   222
   Reading for Ideas: "U.S. Passports Changing
     with Technology," by James L. Roper   222
   Gathering Information   225

PART TWO: LANGUAGE FOR WRITING   225
Citing Authorities   225
   Practicing What You've Learned   227
Paraphrasing   227
   Practicing What You've Learned   228
PART THREE: SYSTEMS FOR WRITING   229
Essay Development   229
   Practicing What You've Learned   231
   Assignments   232
PART FOUR: EVALUATING FOR REWRITING   232

CHAPTER 12

LIVING TOGETHER
ON A SMALL PLANET

237

PART ONE: IDEAS FOR WRITING   238
What is Intelligence?   238
   Brainstorming   241
   Freewriting   242
   Reading for Ideas: "What is Intelligence, Anyway?"
     by Isaac Asimov   242
   Gathering Information   244
PART TWO: LANGUAGE FOR WRITING   244
Summarizing   244
   Citing Sources in Summaries   248
   Practicing What You've Learned   248
PART THREE: SYSTEMS FOR WRITING   249
Introductions and Conclusions   249
   Introductions   249
   Conclusions   251
   Practicing What You've Learned   251
   Assignments   253
PART FOUR: EVALUATING FOR REWRITING   253

PREFACE

MOSAIC: THE PROGRAM

Mosaic consists of eight texts plus two instructor's manuals for in-college or college-bound nonnative English students. *Mosaic I* is for intermediate to high-intermediate students, while *Mosaic II* is for high-intermediate to low-advanced students. Within each level, I and II, the books are carefully coordinated by theme, vocabulary, grammar structure, and, where possible, language functions. A chapter in one book corresponds to and reinforces material taught in the same chapter of the other three books at that level for a truly integrated, four-skills approach.

Each level, I and II, consists of four books plus an instructor's manual. In addition to *A Content-Based Writing Book*, they include:

- *A Content-Based Grammar I, II:* Each grammar chapter relates to a specific theme, so the exercises focus on contexts and ideas. There is a wide variety of comunicative, functional activities.
- *A Reading Skills Book I, II:* Selections in these books come from many sources, including newspapers, magazines, textbooks, and literature. The emphasis is on building reading and study skills; for example, skimming, scanning, determining the author's point of view, reading charts and graphs, guessing the meaning of new words from context, making inferences, outlining, and techniques for remembering what has been read.
- *A Listening-Speaking Skills Book I, II:* Following lectures on chapter themes, the activities and exercises in these books stress learning how to listen, getting the main idea, outlining, taking notes, and other academic skills. Speaking activities based on language functions are also included. A cassette program with instructor's key accompanies each text.
- *Instructor's Manual I, II:* These manuals provide instructions and guidelines for use of the books separately or in any combination to form a program. For each of the core books, there is a separate section with teaching tips and other suggestions. The instructor's manuals also include sample tests.

MOSAIC I:
A CONTENT-BASED WRITING BOOK

An effective writing course for nonnative speakers should develop independent writers through a systematic approach to the writing process. This process trains students to:

- generate and develop ideas
- learn language directly related to the topic
- apply the appropriate rhetorical patterns to a specific writing task, and
- evaluate and revise initial drafts of their work.

Mosaic I: A Content-Based Writing Book focuses on these crucial elements of the writing process.

Each chapter is divided into four parts. The first part, "Ideas for Writing," helps students generate and develop ideas for writing on topics related to the theme of each chapter. This is done through activities that include reacting to photographs, freewriting, reading for ideas, doing research, and class activities.

The second part, "Language for Writing," presents words, expressions, and structures that students need to know and review in order to write about the chapter topic. Through a series of exercises, students practice these in context so that they can integrate them easily into their own writing.

The third section, "Systems for Writing," introduces rhetorical patterns that provide the student with a framework for expressing their ideas, presenting the format the academic writing requires. This section includes explanations, models, and exercises.

The last section, "Evaluating for Rewriting," guides the student through a series of revisions that emphasize the importance of rewriting and help the student improve his or her work. Each evaluation focuses on the particular teaching points of the chapter.

Mosaic I: A Content-Based Writing Book is most effectively used sequentially. Each chapter covers three to five class hours, making the course well-suited to the typical academic semester or quarter.

ACKNOWLEDGMENTS

We would like to thank our colleagues and students at the University of California, Berkeley, for their insights, dedication and enthusiasm. We would especially like to thank Mary McVey Gill of EBI, Patricia K. Werner, and June McKay for inspiration and expertise they gave throughout the development of our book. Thanks also to

Janet Bollow Associates for their work on the design and production of the text. Finally, our thanks to the following reviewers, whose comments, both favorable and critical, were of great value in the development of this text: Tibe Appelstein, Newbury Junior College; Lida Baker, University of California at Los Angeles; Ellen Broselow, State University of New York, Stony Brook; Van Caliandro, Bronx Community College, City University of New York; Ellen Garshick, Georgetown University; Anne Hagiwara, Eastern Michigan University; Nancy Herzfeld-Pipkin, San Diego State University; Patricia Johnson, University of Wisconsin, Green Bay; Gail Kellersberger, University of Houston; Nancy Lay, City College, City University of New York; Tamara Lucas, San Francisco State University and Stanford University; Debra Mathews, University of Akron; Sandra McKay, San Francisco State University; Pamela McPartland, Hunter College, City University of New York; Maryanne O'Brien, University of Houston; Helen Polensek, Oregon State University; Amy Sonka; Stephanie Vandrick, University of San Francisco.

L. B.
M. P.-B.

CHAPTER 1
NEW CHALLENGES

PART ONE

IDEAS FOR WRITING

IMPRESSIONS OF A NEW CULTURE

The following photos are of typical American scenes. Study them carefully and write one or two captions on the lines provided below each one. (A *caption* is a sentence that describes a picture.) Try to express the overall impression each scene gives. In one complete sentence, capture what each photo says about life in the United States. After you have finished, work in small groups and share your captions with your classmates. Remember to describe more than the photo itself; try to make a general statement about Americans and their values.

Example:

In America, the package is sometimes more important than the product. Americans seem to have a lot of choices.

1. _____

_____

2. _____

_____

3. _____

_____

4. _____

_____

5. _____

_____

Brainstorming

Look at the photos again. In small groups, discuss why you chose your caption for each picture. While you are discussing the photos, list as many new words and expressions as you can in the following chart. Remember to focus your discussion on American cultural values.

Verbs	Adjectives	Nouns	Expressions	Other
Example:				
to advertise	capitalistic	commercialism		
to market		consumerism		
		excess		
		choice		
___	___	___	___	___
___	___	___	___	___
___	___	___	___	___
___	___	___	___	___
___	___	___	___	___
___	___	___	___	___
___	___	___	___	___
___	___	___	___	___
___	___	___	___	___
___	___	___	___	___

Freewriting

What were some of the surprising things you saw and experienced during your first few days in the United States or Canada? What seemed particularly different from life in your country? Write about these things for ten minutes without stopping.

Reading for Ideas[1]

Nick, a twenty-three-year-old American, has gone to Paris, France, to study French. He has written a letter to Masao, a Japanese friend back in the United States, describing his impressions of Paris and some of the problems he has encountered adjusting to a new culture. Read his letter and answer the questions that follow.

Prereading Questions

1. What do you know about Paris? Share your information with your classmates.
2. How would a student from your country react to Paris?
3. What would an American's reactions be in Paris?

Adjusting to a New Culture

Paris
September 30, 198_

Dear Masao,

   Thank you for your card. Sorry it's taken me so long to write. I've been spending all my free time wandering around Paris. It's beautiful! There's something interesting to see in every corner of this city: the old buildings, the quaint neighborhoods, and the historical monuments. The weather's been great, too: cool and dry. The trees that line the boulevards are just starting to change color.

   You asked me about some of the aspects of life here that are different from the United States. The most noticeable thing is that there is much more activity in the streets than in the typical U.S. city. People congregate in the open markets, the sidewalk cafés, and the numerous parks and squares. People dress more stylishly and formally, too. Both men and women look as though they spend a lot of time dressing and grooming themselves every day. Then, of course, there's the food. Food seems to be more important here: It's beautifully displayed in <u>charcuterie</u> (delicatessen) windows and in the

---

[1]The selections in the sections "Reading for Ideas" are meant to provide ideas on the chapter topic. Read these selections quickly and do not be concerned with understanding all of the ideas and vocabulary.

markets. Everything's fresher and better tasting than at home, even the food in the student cafeterias. I've gained five pounds since I arrived.

There are a few things that bother me, though. I'm still having a hard time with the language. People speak very fast, and it's hard to get them to repeat things. Also, I keep forgetting when to use the formal "you" (<u>vous</u>) and the informal "you" (<u>tu</u>). It can be insulting if you use the wrong one. People in general are more formal here, and it's hard to make friends. I guess that can be true in any big city in a new country, but the French <u>do</u> seem to be less warm and friendly than the folks back home! The thing that annoys me the most, though, is that people don't line up! At the bank or at the ticket window at the train station, it's <u>first come, first served</u>. It seems that you have to be pretty aggressive just to get your day-to-day business taken care of.

Well, that's about all for now. I know the next time I write I'll be better adjusted to these things. What kinds of problems did you experience when you first came to the United States? How long did it take you to get used to things? Write to me and give me some advice before I decide to turn around and come home.

Take care,

Nick

Postreading Questions

1. Is Nick basically happy or unhappy in Paris? Find examples from the letter to support your answer. _____

2. Why does Nick have trouble with the formal and informal "you" in French? Give an example of a persistent problem that you have with English. Try to explain why it is a problem.

_____

_____

3. Why do you think Nick is having a hard time making friends in Paris? Have you had a difficult time making friends in the United States? _____

4. Why is Nick bothered by the fact that the French don't seem to line up at the bank? How important is lining up in your

country? What aspect (if any) of getting day-to-day business taken care of in the United States is different for you?

_____

_____

5. Nick is planning to stay in Paris for one year. How do you think he'll feel about his experience at the end of the year? Has there been a change in your feelings about life in the United States since you arrived?

_____

_____

Gathering Information

Interview a classmate about his or her problems and experiences adjusting to life in the United States. Include questions about language, making friends, and taking care of day-to-day business. Take notes here:

Interview Notes:

_____

_____

_____

_____

_____

PART TWO

LANGUAGE FOR WRITING

DESCRIBING PEOPLE, PLACES, AND THINGS

Following is a chart showing the language Nick used in his letter to describe his impressions of the people, places, and things in a new culture. Study the words and expressions Nick used, then complete the chart with words and expressions that describe your impressions of the people, places, and things in the United States or Canada.

	People	Places	Things	Other
Nick in France	dress stylishly and formally	quaint neighbor-hoods old buildings historical monuments	food: beautifully displayed fresher and better tasting	
You in the United States or Canada	_____	_____	_____	_____
	_____	_____	_____	_____
	_____	_____	_____	_____
	_____	_____	_____	_____
	_____	_____	_____	_____
	_____	_____	_____	_____
	_____	_____	_____	_____
	_____	_____	_____	_____
	_____	_____	_____	_____
	_____	_____	_____	_____
	_____	_____	_____	_____
	_____	_____	_____	_____

DESCRIBING PROBLEMS

Following is a list of expressions that Nick used to describe his problems in adjusting to life in France. Study them carefully. Then use each expression in a complete sentence describing your own problems adjusting to a new culture. You may need to add other expressions as well. Consider problems with the language, making friends, and conducting day-to-day business. When you have finished, exchange your sentences with a partner.

There are a few things that bother me:

I'm having a hard time with _____

_____ .

It's hard to _____ .

I keep _____ ing _____
                (verb)
and forgetting when to _____

_____ .

People are much more _____

_____ .

The thing that annoys me the most, though, is (that) _____

_____ .

It seems that you have to be pretty _____

just to _____

_____ .

ASKING INFORMATION QUESTIONS

When Nick asked Masao, "What kinds of problems did you experience when you first came to the United States?" what kind of answer was he expecting? When you want more than a simple *yes* or *no*, and when you want a lot of information from someone, you ask information questions. Information questions are those that begin with *who, what, when, where, how,* and *why*. In the following chart make a list of information questions that you might want to ask someone who has arrived here recently. When you finish, share your list with a partner and add any he or she had that you didn't.

Who . . . ?

_____

_____

_____

_____

What . . . ?

_____

_____

_____

_____

_____

When . . . ?

_____

_____

_____

_____

Where . . . ?

_____

_____

_____

_____

How much . . . ?

_____

_____

_____

_____

How many . . . ?

_____

_____

_____

_____

How long . . . ?

_____

_____

_____

_____

Why . . . ?

_____

_____

_____

_____

_____

Practicing What You've Learned

Exercise 1 Using ten of your best questions from the preceding exercise, find a new partner and interview him or her about his or her experiences in the United States or Canada. Take notes on what your partner says.

Notes:

_____

_____

_____

_____

_____

_____

_____

_____

Exercise 2 Go back to the chart you used in "Describing People, Places, and Things" and fill it in for your partner with the words and expressions that describe his or her impressions of the United States or Canada. Use the information that you gathered from your interview.

Exercise 3 Write one paragraph about your partner's experiences as a newcomer to this country based on your interview with him or her.

PART THREE

SYSTEMS FOR WRITING

THE PARAGRAPH

A paragraph is a group of sentences that expresses one idea. A paragraph looks like this:

Notice the *indentation*. When many paragraphs are grouped together, the indentation tells the reader that a new paragraph has begun.

A paragraph can stand alone to express one idea or it can be grouped with other paragraphs, as in an essay. When a paragraph is part of an essay, it still expresses only one idea, but the idea is related to the ideas in all of the other paragraphs. Study this diagram of an essay (you'll see more about the essay in Chapter 8):

A paragraph usually begins with a sentence that expresses the main idea (called the *topic sentence*). It contains points that *support* the main idea, and examples that illustrate these points. Another characteristic of a paragraph is that all of the sentences relate to the main idea expressed in the first sentence. This is called *unity*. Finally, each sentence in a paragraph connects smoothly to the sentence before and after it. This is called *coherence*. You will learn more about *topic sentences, paragraph support, unity,* and *coherence* in Chapters 1 through 7.

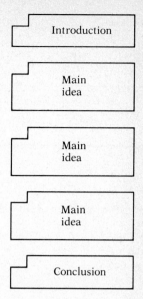

THE TOPIC SENTENCE

The sentence that expresses the main idea of a paragraph is called the *topic sentence*. Just as a caption describes the essence of a photograph, the topic sentence captures the main idea of a paragraph. One characteristic of a topic sentence is that it contains only *one idea*. This is because the purpose of a paragraph is to discuss only one idea. Compare these topic sentences:

a. Moving to another country is often difficult because you don't have your family and friends around you.

b. Moving to another country is often difficult because you don't have your friends around you and you have to communicate in a new language.

Notice that Sentence **a** contains only one main idea ("you don't have your family and friends around you"). Sentence **b** has two ideas ("you don't have your friends around you," and "you have to communicate in a new language"). Therefore, Sentence **a** is the better topic sentence. Sentence **b** has too many ideas to be discussed in one paragraph.

Now, read the following pair of topic sentences and select the better one. Which one has only one idea?

a. The French are famous for their love of liberty, equality, and brotherhood.

b. The French are famous for their love of liberty.

Sentence **b** is the better topic sentence because it contains only one idea. Discussing the ideas in Sentence **a** probably would require more than one paragraph.

Another characteristic of a topic sentence is that it *focuses* on an *aspect* of a topic. That is, it expresses the writer's attitude or approach to the topic. This is similar to the way a photographer selects one object in a scene and focuses the camera on it. Focusing a camera on every object in a scene is impossible, so the photographer chooses the most interesting or important one. Similarly, it is impossible to focus on many aspects of a subject in one essay, so the writer chooses the most interesting or important aspect. Compare these topic sentences:

a. It is difficult to learn a second language as an adult.

b. It is difficult to learn a second language as an adult because adults are more self-conscious than children.

Sentence **b** is better than Sentence **a** because it focuses on one aspect of the topic of adult second-language learning. Sentence **a** is unfocused; it suggests the entire topic of adult second-language learning. It needs to be narrowed down.

One way to make a topic sentence more focused is to ask an information question about the topic: *who? what? when? where? why?* or *how?* For example, in the topic sentences you just saw, the writer states *why* it is difficult to learn a second language as an adult. *Why?* and *how?* are often the most useful questions to ask. To practice, rewrite the following unfocused topic sentences by asking an information question about each one. Possible question words are given for the first three; you think of question words for the last three. (Don't forget that a topic sentence must also contain only one main idea!)

1. American culture is different from my culture. (*How?* or *in what way?*)

2. It is easy to make friends in a new country. (*Why?, in what way?* or *how?*)

3. Many Americans like French food. (*Why?*)

4. American tourists in Europe are easy to identify.

5. Many foreign students are unprepared for culture shock.

6. People from all countries are traveling more and more these days.

The third characteristic of the topic sentence is that it tells the reader *exactly* what the paragraph is about. The reader should be able to read a good topic sentence and *predict* what the rest of the paragraph will be about before he or she reads it. In this way, the writer establishes a good relationship with the reader by helping him or her know what to expect. Try this: Read the following topic sentence. Write down in note form what you think the paragraph is about, then go on and read the rest of the paragraph.

Topic Sentence:

The one aspect of French culture that many Americans have little difficulty adjusting to is the cuisine.

What the paragraph is probably about: _____

_____

The Rest of the Paragraph:

In fact, many Americans go to France specifically to sample its excellent cuisine. This is because the appearance and taste of French food are highly celebrated throughout the world, and the ingredients are not foreign to the American palate. As a matter of fact, though many Americans have difficulty with the French language, they often know a smattering of French food terms, such as *pâté, soufflé, quiche,* and *croissant*. Although Americans visiting France may have a difficult time speaking French and making close friends, they rarely have difficulty with the food.

Now, compare your prediction with what the paragraph was actually about. Was your prediction correct?

Compare the topic sentence you just saw with the following:

There is one aspect of French culture that Americans have little difficulty adjusting to.

This topic sentence is too *general* and too *vague* (look these words up in your dictionary), so it doesn't give you a clear picture of what the paragraph is about. To summarize, a good topic sentence:

1. expresses one main idea
2. is focused
3. tells the reader what the paragraph is about

Practicing What You've Learned

Exercise 1 The following paragraphs discuss American cultural preferences about body contact, personal attractiveness, and social activities. Practice identifying topic sentences by reading the paragraphs and answering the questions that follow.

a. English speakers generally avoid body contact when they speak to each other. Usually, they will not even touch each other with their hands. When they are forced to stand close together— for example, in an elevator—their muscles are tense, they avoid looking directly at each other, and they are silent. Even husbands and wives generally do not touch in public.[2]

1. What is the main idea?
2. Where is it expressed?
3. Underline it.

b. Every culture has its standards for personal attractiveness. Nigerians think plumpness is attractive, whereas Americans prefer slenderness. In France, a man looks attractive wearing a jacket over his shoulders, with his arms out of the sleeves; in America, the same man dressed this way would look feminine. People in some cultures like natural body smells; people in others, including Americans, do not.[3]

1. What is the main idea?
2. Where is it expressed?
3. Underline it.

c. The emphasis Americans give to time in social activities seems extreme to some foreigners. Many Americans, for example, believe that church services should start at exactly 11:00 A.M. and end by 12:00; ministers have been dismissed for preaching too long. School dances must end at 10:00 P.M., even though the boys and girls are behaving themselves and having a wonderful time. Restaurants are sometimes judged by the speed of their service, rather than the quality of their food.[4]

1. What is the main idea?
2. Where is it expressed?
3. Underline it.

Exchange answers with a partner. Were the main ideas expressed in the same place in each paragraph?

Exercise 2 Although the topic sentence can be found almost anywhere in a paragraph written by a native speaker, in the

---

[2]Adapted from Gregory A. Barnes, *Communication Skills for the Foreign-Born Professional* (Philadelphia: ISI Press, 1982), p. 11.

[3]Adapted from Barnes, *Communication Skills for the Foreign-Born Professional*, p. 13.

[4]Adapted from Barnes, *Communication Skills for the Foreign-Born Professional*, p. 10.

paragraphs you will be writing in this course, the topic sentence will be at the beginning. You should have underlined the first sentences of Paragraphs **a, b,** and **c** in Exercise 1. Now reread the topic sentences in Exercise 1 and complete the following chart.

Paragraph	a		b		c	
	YES	**NO**	**YES**	**NO**	**YES**	**NO**
The topic sentence contains only one idea.	____	____	____	____	____	____
The topic sentence focuses on an aspect of the topic.	____	____	____	____	____	____
The topic sentence tells the reader what the paragraph is about.	____	____	____	____	____	____

Exercise 3   These exercises will help you recognize the elements of a good topic sentence and teach you how to incorporate them into your writing. The following paragraphs need topic sentences. First, read each paragraph and list all of the supporting ideas it contains. This will help you understand what each paragraph is about. Then, choose the best topic sentence from the three possibilities given. You may want to refer to the questions in the chart you completed in Exercise 2. Go over your answers in class.

Example:

In fact, many Americans go to France specifically to sample its excellent cuisine. This is because the appearance and taste of French food are highly celebrated throughout the world, and the ingredients are not foreign to the American palate. As a matter of fact, though many Americans have difficulty with the French language, they often know a smattering of French food terms, such as *pâté, soufflé, quiche,* and *croissant.* Although Americans visiting France may have a difficult time speaking French and making close friends, they rarely have difficulty with the food.

Supporting Ideas:

Americans go to France because of its cuisine.
French cuisine isn't foreign to Americans. They know
food terms. Even though they may have trouble
with some aspects of French culture, they like
the food.

Topic Sentences:

1. Many Americans have difficulty adjusting to French culture.
2. Many Americans understand French food terms.
(3.) The one aspect of French culture that many Americans have little difficulty adjusting to is the cuisine.

   a. In introductions as well as in general conversations, speakers maintain frequent eye contact. That is, they look directly at each other. Most people become nervous if there is too much eye contact: This is called *staring*. When shaking hands, people shake firmly and *briefly*. The expression "He shakes hands like a dead fish" refers to a limp or weak handshake, a sign in the American culture of a weak character. Prolonged handshaking is not unusual.[5]

Supporting Ideas:

_____

_____

_____

Topic Sentences:

1. Direct eye contact is important during introductions in the United States.
2. In America, limp handshakes are a sign of weak character.
3. Direct eye contact and firm handshakes during introductions are customary in the United States.

   b. A few days in the home of a friendly family can help the student make the change to a new environment. A host family can help the student learn about American customs and family life and about social and cultural activities in the community. Most importantly, the host family can be friends in the commu-

---

[5]Adapted from Deena R. Levine and Mara B. Adelman, *Beyond Language: Intercultural Communication for English as a Second Language* (Englewood Cliffs, N.J.: Prentice-Hall, 1982).

nity to which the student may turn in the difficult period of cultural adjustment. The relationship may be equally valuable for the participating family. By hosting an international student, family members can increase their knowledge and awareness of another culture and country.[6]

Supporting Ideas:

_____

_____

Topic Sentences:

1. Arriving in a foreign country can be a lonely and bewildering time for a new student from abroad.

2. Because being a new foreign student can be a lonely and difficult experience, staying with a host family is helpful and comforting.

3. A host family can learn a great deal about foreign people and their cultures by offering hospitality to a foreign student.

   c. The most common problem foreign students face in adjusting to a new culture is an "identity crisis." The identity crisis occurs when the student is forced to consider who he or she really is. The difficulty in this comes from the personality changes the student may go through caused by a new environment. The student must adapt his or her old self to a new situation, and this results in personality changes. He or she may have to play a different role in this new environment. The process can be difficult, but if the student is aware of this problem, he or she can usually overcome it.[7]

Supporting Ideas:

_____

_____

_____

---

[6]Adapted from Jim Leonard, "Design for a One-Day Host Family Workshop," *Readings in Intercultural Communication* 5 (Pittsburgh, Pa.: The Intercultural Communications Network, 1976), p. 30.

[7]Adapted from Jerry Wilcox, James O'Driscoll, Nobleza Asuncion-Lande, and Cal Downs, "Models for Re-Entry Transition Seminars and Workshops," *Readings in Intercultural Communication* 5 (Pittsburgh, Pa.: The Intercultural Communications Network, 1976), p. 173.

Topic Sentences:

1. It has long been recognized that when people move between cultures, certain problems of adaptation are bound to occur.

2. There are many problems a foreign student faces when leaving his or her country, such as finding a place to live and learning the way around town.

3. People face problems throughout life, and a foreign student is no exception.

Exercise 4   In this exercise, you will read five topic sentences. For each of these, predict what you expect to read in the paragraph. Make notes about your predictions and then compare your notes with a partner's.

Example:

Most people live for a long time in a new culture before they can relax and accept what they see around them.

The new culture is different. The foreigner is nervous, intimidated, and confused at first. Examples:
College registration procedures are bureaucratic, complicated. With time, one becomes accustomed to things, accepts them, and sees benefits.

1. Some very funny things happened to me during my first few days in the United States, but the most comical was our night in a Boston restaurant.

   _____

   _____

   _____

   _____

2. I am the product of two cultures, and I have adopted the desirable aspects of each culture without feeling guilt or conflict.

   _____

   _____

   _____

   _____

   _____

3. Moving to another culture is often a difficult step because you usually do not have family and friends around for emotional support.

_____

_____

_____

_____

_____

4. Although American informality is well known, many people interpret it as a lack of respect.

_____

_____

_____

_____

5. One benefit of foreign travel is the realization that you have a great deal in common with people of other cultures.

_____

_____

_____

_____

Exercise 5   The topic sentences from Exercise 3 that you did not choose were not good because they either: (1) had more than one idea, (2) were not focused, or (3) didn't tell you what the paragraph was about. Read the sentences from Exercise 3 that were not good topic sentences and explain _why_. Refer to the points just listed.

Paragraph a:

Sentence 1 _____

Sentence 2 _____

Sentence 3 is an appropriate topic sentence.

Paragraph b:

Sentence 1 _____

Sentence 2 is an appropriate topic sentence.

Sentence 3 _____

Paragraph c:

Sentence 1 is an appropriate topic sentence.

Sentence 2 _____

Sentence 3 _____

Exercise 6 In this exercise, you are going to write topic sentences for the following paragraphs. As you did in Exercise 3, make a list of all the supporting ideas in each paragraph before you write the topic sentence. Be sure your topic sentences have one main idea, are focused, and tell the reader what the paragraph is about.

a. _____

_____

For example, North Americans do not prolong eye contact during a conversation, whereas South Americans do. A person from North America usually meets the other person's eyes for a few seconds, looks away, and then back again, but a South American looks directly into the other person's eyes and considers it impolite not to do so. Another difference is the contrast in using hand movements while speaking. The South American uses many gestures. The North American, however, uses them only occasionally. The North and South American have more in common when we examine the distance each maintains from the person he or she is talking with. Unless a close friendship exists, both the North and the South American stand about two to three feet from one another. By studying the differences in body language of a group of North and South Americans, we could probably figure out where each person comes from.[8]

Supporting Ideas:

_____

_____

_____

b. _____

_____

In Paris one can recognize Americans two hundred yards away simply by the way they walk. A French student told me that when he returned home after three months at the Harvard

[8]Adapted from Wilcox et al., *Readings in Intercultural Communication* 5, p. 15.

Business School, his father was shocked when he saw his son walk from the plane. "You've become an American," were his first words of greeting. "You bounce when you walk!" An American often walks with swinging arms and a rolling pelvis as though moving through a space unlimited by human or physical obstacles.[9]

Supporting Ideas:

_____

_____

_____

c. _____

_____

A common example is the gesture of waving farewell. In Italy the palm of the hand is held toward the speaker and the fingers make the motion of drawing the departing person back. In Spain the movement is the same, but the hand is held horizontally. In France the palm is frequently held facing the departing person, and the movement of the hand appears to push the departing person on his way. Some scholars think that exposing one's palm indicates surrender; so perhaps the French form of farewell implies a reassurance of nonaggression. Americans are inclined to show the palm also and move the flattened hand from left to right.[10]

Supporting Ideas:

_____

_____

_____

Getting Started

Most writers create topic sentences after deciding what a paragraph will be about. They do not write the topic sentence before they know what they want to communicate to the reader. You, too, should try to organize your thoughts and focus on one main idea *before* writing a topic sentence. That is, you should know what

---

[9]From Lawrence Wylie, *Beaux Gestes: A Guide to French Body Talk* (Cambridge, Mass.: 1977), The Undergraduate Press, p. xi.

[10]From Wylie, *Beaux Gestes: A Guide to French Body Talk*, p. xiii.

you want to communicate to the reader *before* you write a topic sentence. The following exercises will teach you how to write a topic sentence. Study the steps and the example paragraph, then fill in the spaces for your own response to the following assignment.

Assignments

1. Write a paragraph about the initial impressions a foreigner may have of a new culture.

Nick's Paragraph:

There are some aspects of life in France that are different from life in the United States. For example, there is much more activity in the streets of Paris than in the typical city in the United States. People congregate in the open markets, the sidewalk cafés, and the numerous parks and squares. Also, people dress more stylishly and formally in France, especially in Paris. Both men and women look as though they spend a lot of time dressing and grooming themselves every day. Another noticeable difference is the relative importance of food. It is beautifully displayed in *charcuterie* (delicatessen) windows and in the markets. Everything is fresher and better tasting than in the United States, even the food in the student cafeterias.

Step 1 Make a list of all the things that impressed you when you first came to a new culture. Refer to the freewriting exercise you did in Part One.

Nick Men and women are always well dressed.

People talk fast.   Food is important.
The cars are smaller.   Lots of people are in the streets.
People are formal.   People always seem to be in a hurry.

You _____

_____

_____

_____

_____

_____

_____

Step 2 Now look closely at your list and decide what all the ideas have in common. Eliminate unrelated items. This step helps you form the main idea of the paragraph.

Nick Men and women are always well dressed.

Not different from U.S.

~~People talk~~ fast.   Food is important.

~~The cars are smaller.~~   Lots of people are in the streets.
Not very important

People are formal.   ~~People always seem to be in~~ a hurry.

The rest are aspects of life that are really different.   *Not really different from the U.S.*

Why do you think Nick crossed out "People talk fast," "The cars are smaller," and "People always seem to be in a hurry"?

You _____

_____

_____

_____

_____

_____

Step 3 Write a topic sentence that describes the theme you found in Step 2. This step is like writing a caption for a photograph. Refer to the information on the topic sentence on p. 13.

Nick There are a lot of aspects of life in France that are very different.

You _____

_____

_____

_____

_____

_____

Step 4 Exchange papers with a partner or with your teacher and have him or her check to see that your sentence relates to all the items in Step 2. Check to see that your sentence has one main idea, is focused on an aspect of the topic, and tells the reader what the paragraph is about.

Nick   There are a lot of aspects of life in France that are very different.

Notice that Nick's first attempt at a topic sentence has problems: It's not focused, and it doesn't really tell the reader what the paragraph is about. It's too *general* and *vague*.

Here's Nick's new topic sentence:

There are some aspects of life in France that are different from the United States.

You _____

_____

_____

_____

_____

_____

Step 5   Now complete your paragraph, remembering to include all the supporting ideas suggested by your topic sentence. Include specific examples to support and develop your topic sentence.

2. Write a paragraph about your problems adjusting to life in the United States or Canada. Refer to Nick's letter and go through Steps 1 through 5 for writing a topic sentence.

3. Write a paragraph about possible problems one could encounter adjusting to life in the United States or Canada. Refer to your interview in Part One.

4. Choose one of the photographs in Part One and write a paragraph about the aspect of American culture it shows.

PART FOUR

EVALUATING FOR REWRITING

The final and most important stage of writing is evaluating what you have written and rewriting it. As a help to you in evaluating your own writing, the last section of each chapter will contain exercises to teach you what to look for before rewriting your papers. First you will exchange papers and evaluate a classmate's writing. Later you will answer some questions about your own paragraph.

Working with Your Partner

Exchange paragraphs with your partner and use the following questionnaire to evaluate the assignments in this chapter.

1. Just read the topic sentence (without reading the rest of the paragraph) and copy it here:

   _____

   _____

   _____

   _____

2. How many ideas does it express? _____

   If the answer is *more than one,* stop and tell your partner to rewrite the topic sentence. If the answer is *one,* go on to Question 3.

3. Is the topic sentence *focused?*

   Yes _____   No _____

   If the answer is *no,* stop and tell your partner to rewrite the topic sentence. If the answer is *yes,* go on to Question 4.

4. What do you expect to read about in the paragraph, given your partner's topic sentence? Write the ideas here:

   _____

   _____

   _____

   _____

5. Now read the paragraph.
   Was your prediction accurate?

   Yes _____   No _____

   If the answer is *yes,* go on to Question 6. If the answer is *no,* give the paper back to your partner so he or she can rewrite the paragraph.

6. Are there any ideas that are not suggested by the topic sentences? That is, are there any irrelevant ideas that should be eliminated?

   Yes _____   No _____

   If the answer is *yes,* eliminate the irrelevant sentences. If the answer is *no,* congratulate your partner!

Working on Your Own

Now you should be ready to evaluate your own paper. Go through the questions again. Take into consideration what your partner said about your paper when he or she evaluated it. Is there more to add? Things to eliminate? Words to change?

If your topic sentence expresses only one main idea and if all your sentences clearly relate to that idea, congratulations! You have written a good paragraph.

CHAPTER 2
ACADEMIC LIFE

PART ONE

IDEAS FOR WRITING

ISSUES IN EDUCATION

College students have opinions on many subjects, but they are often the most vocal about issues that affect them directly: issues in education. You and your classmates may be concerned about many of these issues at your school: Are lecture classes too large and impersonal? Is the atmosphere too competitive? Are your instructors really helping you learn? Is your major preparing you for a career? Consider your own opinions about these issues in education as you read the following statements collected from a variety of people who work and study at American colleges and universities.

1. *Gloria (first-year student)*: "I like seminar classes best because I can really learn in a small class. Those huge lecture classes are a waste of time."

2. *David (second-year student)*: "Although my parents want me to continue at the university and get an advanced degree, I'm anxious to get a job and gain some work experience."

3. *Alice (college admissions officer)*: "The more people who have access to education, the better. I don't agree with the system that reserves education only for a few and uses the majority of the population as a work force."

4. *Eric (computer science major)*: "I can't understand why I have to study English literature and world history. I won't need those courses to become a computer scientist."

5. *Karen (English major)*: "I majored in the humanities because I thought I would learn more about people and life than if I majored in biology or chemistry."

6. *Ted (faculty member)*: "As a professor, I like to think of myself more as a consultant than an authority figure."

7. *Marta (immigrant student accounting major)*: "Education is worthwhile only insofar as it prepares students for a profession."

8. *Bernard (foreign student)*: "Learning is best when everyone helps each other out in a cooperative atmosphere."

Read the statements again with a classmate. For each one, decide what the opposing viewpoint is. Then give the argument a general name. In other words, what is the *issue?* Provide this information in the chart below. The first one is done for you.

Who said it?	What did he or she say?	What's the opposing point of view?	What's the point of disagreement?
Gloria	Seminars are better than lectures.	Lecture classes are better.	Seminars versus lectures
⎯⎯	⎯⎯	⎯⎯	⎯⎯
⎯⎯	⎯⎯	⎯⎯	⎯⎯
⎯⎯	⎯⎯	⎯⎯	⎯⎯
⎯⎯	⎯⎯	⎯⎯	⎯⎯
⎯⎯	⎯⎯	⎯⎯	⎯⎯
⎯⎯	⎯⎯	⎯⎯	⎯⎯
⎯⎯	⎯⎯	⎯⎯	⎯⎯
⎯⎯	⎯⎯	⎯⎯	⎯⎯
⎯⎯	⎯⎯	⎯⎯	⎯⎯
⎯⎯	⎯⎯	⎯⎯	⎯⎯
⎯⎯	⎯⎯	⎯⎯	⎯⎯
⎯⎯	⎯⎯	⎯⎯	⎯⎯
⎯⎯	⎯⎯	⎯⎯	⎯⎯
⎯⎯	⎯⎯	⎯⎯	⎯⎯

Go over your chart with one or two classmates. Are the points of disagreement you listed in the fourth column the same? Do these same points of disagreement exist in your culture? List any additional educational issues in the space at the bottom of the chart.

Brainstorming

1. Write any new words or expressions from the statements in "Issues in Education" in the following space. Consult a classmate or your dictionary to learn their meanings.

   _____

   _____

2. Look at your list of arguments from "Issues in Education." Create a vocabulary list by making notes in the following chart about each side of the conflict. Write as many new words and expressions for each point of disagreement as you can. Exchange with a classmate and add his or her new words to your list. The first one is done for you.

Argument: *Seminars versus Lectures*

| a waste of time | pressure | impersonal |
| seminar | cooperation | anonymous |

Argument: _____

_____

_____

Argument: _____

_____

_____

Argument: _____

_____

_____

Argument: _____

_____

_____

Argument: _____

_____

_____

Argument: _____

_____

_____

Argument: _____

_____

_____

Freewriting

Choose one of the issues in education you've been discussing. Write about this issue for ten minutes without stopping.

Reading for Ideas

Prereading Questions

The following essay, written by Thomas Patrick Melady, president of an American university, appeared in the opinion section of a college newspaper. Melady is concerned about the relationship between teachers and students. Before you read the essay, answer the following questions.

1. In your opinion, should college faculty members and administrators be available to help students with academic and personal problems outside of class? Why or why not?

2. Do the faculty members and administrators at your school seem to be willing to help you with your academic and personal problems outside of class?

Losing Sight of Students

As a university president, I feel that there is a serious danger in higher education today. We administrators are failing to meet our responsibilities because in our well-meaning but time-consuming efforts to achieve financial stability, we are losing sight of human needs in the university experience. We are failing to spend the time 5 to develop meaningful relationships with students. This is our most basic responsibility, and I believe that this problem deserves our immediate attention.

People need people. In all that I read in the newspapers, the educational journals, the prestigious foundation reports, I see very 10 little attention being paid to the primary responsibility of educators—the student. Somehow, amid the budget reports and the frantic trips to state capitals and to Washington seeking financial assistance, the student was forgotten.

As the pressures increase in the coming decade, I believe the real danger to higher education is depersonalization. A serious concern is that presidents and deans will turn themselves into vague shadows on our campuses, into tarnished bureaucrats with no time in their busy schedules to meet with students. And I am not talking about just "availability" here. I mean we need to make time to develop deep personal relationships that will remain beyond the four short years of a university education.

Before it is too late, I think we need to ask ourselves this question: What is happening to the dream we once cherished about higher education? That we could receive young people at the critical age of young adulthood and play a major role in their maturation, in developing their cultural and intellectual curiosity, in helping them acquire a healthy sense of values? What happened to our role as counselors, as guides on the path to the good life?

Time. A simple four-letter word. I hear it constantly in the halls and boardrooms of academe. Nobody has any time. Our lives accelerate at such a rapid pace, we have no time even to say hello and goodbye. We rush here and there, and we don't even know one another. And when we reach that point, when we finally come face to face with the stranger who is supposed to be our friend, then we no longer can claim to call ourselves a community. When that time comes—and it is almost here—we have lost an important part of the vision of higher education.

I beg presidents, deans, and faculty members to refuse to become part of this growing cancer of depersonalization. The students are ready for us. In this era of compromised values, where we see everywhere the results of the breakdown of traditional structures, where we witness on a grand scale the impact of our highly mechanistic society with its lack of leadership and a sense of fear and separateness, our students are saying: "We need your guidance, we need you; we need someone who cares."

In spite of the mounting pressures we administrators face, we must recognize once and for all that students are our highest priority. As our time becomes increasingly scarce, we must stop ourselves, stand back to gain some perspective, recognize our weaknesses; and then we must make the tremendous effort to take more time from our overcrowded schedules and spend it with our students.

We need to show our students we care. This is a primary responsibility of university presidents, and we must send out the message: Our students are our first concern.

Thomas Patrick Melady, *The Daily Californian,* November 11, 1980, p. 9.

Postreading Questions

1. What is the author's point of view?

   _____

   _____

   _____

   _____

2. What reasons does he give to support his point of view?

   _____

   _____

   _____

   _____

3. Is there an *opposing* point of view? If so, what is it? Who might have this point of view, and why?

   _____

   _____

   _____

   _____

4. In the chart below, list the advantages and disadvantages of college administrators and faculty members taking the time to develop closer relationships with their students. You may find some in the essay, and you may have to think of your own.

Advantages	Disadvantages

Gathering Information

Choose the statement from "Issues in Education" that most closely reflects your own point of view. Now paraphrase the statement in a short sentence. Make up a questionnaire like the following one and ask two classmates and three Americans (out of class) to fill in the questionnaire.

QUESTIONNAIRE

Statement (paraphrase the statement you agree with; for example, "Professors should be consultants rather than authority figures.") _

_____

_____

Name _____

Age _____

Male   Female   (circle one)

Occupation _____

Do you agree or disagree with the statement above? _____

Please write below as many advantages as you can to the educational issue presented in the statement.

1. _____

_____

2. _____

_____

3. _____

_____

4. _____

_____

5. _____

_____

PART TWO

LANGUAGE FOR WRITING

STATING ADVANTAGES AND DISADVANTAGES

Gloria and Ted are discussing whether small classes are better than large classes. Gloria prefers seminars and is listing their advantages, whereas Ted sees more advantages to large classes. As you read what they say, pay particular attention to the italicized words and expressions, which are useful in describing either advantages or disadvantages of an issue.

Here's what Gloria said about small classes: "There are many advantages to seminars. They

- *encourage* close teacher–student relationships
- *enable* all the students in class to participate
- *provide* a more personal atmosphere
- *make it possible* for students to know each other
- *are conducive* to cooperative learning."

Here's what Ted said about large classes: "Here are some advantages to lectures. They

- *allow* students to take responsibility for their own learning
- *create* a formal learning setting
- *promote* independence and competition, which
- *prepare* students for life after graduation from college."

As Marta heard Gloria and Ted talking, she thought of disadvantages to both seminars and lectures. Here's what she said: "Both seminars and lectures have disadvantages. While lecture classes *inhibit* close relationships between students, seminars *lead* to a situation where there is too much contact between teachers and students. This *results* in a lack of respect for faculty and *prevents* students from taking their studies seriously. While seminars *condone* laziness on the part of the students, lectures *discourage* real learning."

Practicing What You've Learned

Write sentences that express your feelings about the following issues. Try to use all of the words and expressions in the preceding exercise at least once.

- seminars versus lectures
- education for professional training versus education for self-fulfillment
- education for the masses versus education for a few
- humanities versus the sciences
- broad education versus specialization
- teacher as consultant versus teacher as authority figure
- cooperative learning versus competitive learning

PART THREE

SYSTEMS FOR WRITING

PARAGRAPH UNITY

In Chapter 1, you saw that every paragraph has a topic sentence that expresses one main idea. You also saw that the topic sentence must focus on an aspect of the topic and that it must tell the reader exactly what the paragraph is about. In this chapter, you will learn the importance of *unity* in a paragraph. A paragraph that is *unified* is one in which all the sentences relate to and develop the topic sentence. Read the following two paragraphs. Which one best illustrates the principle of unity?

a. Studies have shown that community college students tend to learn more in introductory courses than students at four-year colleges. There are many reasons for this. One is that introductory humanities and science courses such as psychology and biology are usually much smaller at community colleges than at the typical four-year college. As a result, community college students often get more attention from their instructors. Another reason more real learning may take place in community college courses is that the instructors tend to be more dedicated to teaching: They are not required to do research and to publish books and articles as are tenured four-year college professors. Consequently, they have more time to devote to preparing lessons, grading papers, and meeting with students. These are just a few of the reasons that community college students often learn more than their counterparts at four-year colleges.

b. Most schools and colleges have counseling services that help students choose the appropriate courses for their majors and plan their careers. The services usually consist of counselors who see students individually or in small groups. In individual or group sessions, students, with the aid of a trained counselor, determine their academic and career goals. These services also provide aptitude, interest, personality, and achievement tests to help students learn more about their interests and abilities. There are also psychologists and therapists who help students with particular difficulties such as emotional disturbances or learning problems. In addition, health examinations as well as nursing and medical services are available in most schools. Therefore, students at most schools and colleges have many resources to help them make important academic and career choices.

If you said that Paragraph **a** is an example of a unified paragraph, you were correct. Paragraph **b** is *not* unified. Can you explain why it isn't? In Paragraph **b**, there are sentences that have nothing to do with the idea expressed in the topic sentence. In Paragraph **a**, every sentence is related to the topic sentence.

Sometimes you may write paragraphs that aren't quite unified; this happens to good writers, too. It's a natural part of the writing process: You have many good ideas that you want to get down on paper, but they may not be appropriate for your topic. When this happens, reread your paragraph and eliminate the unrelated ideas. The following exercise will help you practice this important editing process. Reread Paragraph **b.** Locate the irrelevant sentences and cross them out. Then, if you think it is necessary, add a few new sentences to the paragraph that further develop the topic sentence. When you finish, you should have a complete, unified paragraph.

Practicing What You've Learned

Exercise 1   Practice what you've learned about unity by editing the following paragraphs. Read each one carefully. Make sure you understand the main idea as expressed in the topic sentence, then cross out any irrelevant sentences.

a. (1) Many college and university students in the United States find it necessary to work while attending school in order to support themselves and pay tuition. (2) Some students qualify for "work-study" grants. (3) These are paid positions offered by the college or university to students who demonstrate financial need. (4) Work-study grants are often for positions in the school cafeteria or library. (5) A variety of grants and scholarships are available to qualified applicants from families that could not otherwise afford a college education. (6) Other students whose family income may be too high to qualify for work-study grants have to find part-time jobs on their own in the community. (7) Although part-time work puts extra pressure on college students, many report that the experience actually helps them deal with academic demands.

b. (1) Many students in the United States live away from home while attending college. (2) In some cases, students choose colleges that are many miles away from their home town; some even go to schools on the other side of the country. (3) In this case, they must live apart from their families. (4) Some young people choose to leave home at the age of eighteen even though they are not attending college. (5) Even students who attend colleges in their own towns may sometimes decide to live in apartments or dormitories on campus. (6) Reasonably priced housing has become increasingly hard to find in many college communities. (7) Students who choose to live on campus rather than at home often do so because they want to be involved in campus activities. (8) Some also feel that living close to campus makes them study harder because they are away from the distractions of home life. (9) In general, it is more common for American college students to live on campus than at home.

Exercise 2   In this exercise, you are going to practice developing a unified paragraph from notes on a particular topic. Remember how Nick eliminated irrelevant ideas for his paragraph on life in France in Chapter 1? Follow his procedure. Eliminating irrelevant ideas from notes is an important part of the writing process.

Read and make sure you understand the topic that the notes are for. Then read the notes carefully and cross out any ideas that don't relate to the topic. After that, write a topic sentence that has one main idea, is focused, and tells the reader what the paragraph is about. Finally, write a unified paragraph that supports your topic sentence. To do this, you may need to add ideas of your own on the topic. When you finish each paragraph, read it carefully. Double-check it to see that all sentences relate to and develop your topic sentence.

Paragraph a:

Topic: Advantages and disadvantages of the pass/fail system of evaluation (in place of the traditional grading system)

Notes:

▪ Students are under less pressure when not worrying about grades; they learn more as a result.

- Students don't learn as much in large universities as they do in smaller colleges.
- Students are encouraged to cooperate rather than compete with each other when grades aren't given.
- In schools where grades aren't given, students are lazy; they don't learn as much.
- The ratio of students to teachers should be ten to one for optimal learning to take place.
- With the traditional grading system, grades become more important than the subject matter to be learned.

Paragraph b:

Topic: Advantages of interrupting one's academic career to work full time

Notes:

- College is not the "real world."
- Quitting school temporarily to work makes students appreciate their studies more when they return.
- If students quit school temporarily, they may find it difficult to return to their studies.
- The purpose of higher education is for personal enrichment; quitting school to work full time defeats this purpose.
- Interrupting college to work ultimately helps students choose realistic, profession-oriented majors.
- Young people should take advantage of the opportunity to devote themselves to studying, instead of working.

PARAGRAPH ORGANIZATION: *TBER*

Paragraph organization is putting all the sentences of a paragraph in a logical order. There are many different ways to organize ideas in a paragraph; the order you choose usually depends on the subject you are going to discuss. In this chapter, you are going to learn a basic way of organizing ideas in a paragraph that can be used with a variety of topics. It's called the *TBER* system: *T*opic sentence, *B*ridge, *E*xample, *R*eturn.

In a TBER paragraph, the main idea is clearly expressed in the first sentence (the topic sentence). The second sentence is an explanation of the first sentence, or it may be a "bridge" that leads the reader from the main idea to the supporting examples that will follow. The main part of the paragraph (or "body") consists of three-to-four well-chosen examples that support and relate to the topic sentence. The last sentence is usually a restatement of the main idea/topic sentence.

You'll see other examples of paragraph organization in Chapters 3, 5, 7, and 10.

A TBER paragraph looks like this:

I. **Topic sentence:** Expresses your main idea
II. **Bridge:** Elaborates on your main idea or leads into your examples
III. **Examples:** Support your main idea with concrete evidence, facts, details, etc.
    A. Example 1
    B. Example 2
    C. Example 3, etc.
IV. **Restatement:** Restates your main idea using similar words and phrases

Practice recognizing the parts of a TBER paragraph by reading the following paragraphs and answering the questions that follow.

a. Colleges and universities in the United States and Canada offer a wide variety of subjects. Students can sample different fields of knowledge, but usually major (concentrate) in one field during the last two years of college. If they wish, they may obtain professional training at the undergraduate level—for example, in accounting, teaching, journalism, or chemistry. Certain colleges specialize in training agricultural experts and engineers. For those who wish to prepare for careers in the arts, there are private music schools and fine arts academies. These examples illustrate the variety of courses open to American college and university students.[1]

1. Where is the topic sentence? Underline it. Does it contain the main idea?
2. Is there an explanatory sentence that follows it?
3. How many examples are there in the paragraph?
4. Does the last sentence in the paragraph restate the main idea?

b. A college community is an interesting and lively place. Students become involved in many different activities—social, religious, political, and athletic. Among the activities are college newspapers, musical organizations, dramatic clubs, and political groups. Some of these have faculty advisors. Many religious groups have their own meeting places where services and social activities can be held. Student groups plan activities of all types—from formal dances to picnics. Most colleges have a

[1] Adapted from Ethel and Martin Tiersky, *Customs and Institutions: A Survey of American Culture and Traditions* (New York: Regents Publishing Co., 1975), pp. 155-56.

student union where students can get together for lunch, study sessions, club meetings, and socializing. It's easy to see that American college students are occupied by much more than just their studies.[2]

1. What is the main idea of this paragraph? Where is it expressed?
2. What is the function of the second sentence in the paragraph?
3. What are the functions of the third, fourth, fifth, sixth, and seventh sentences in the paragraph? How does the information in these sentences relate to the main idea?
4. What is the purpose of the last sentence in the paragraph?

Practicing What You've Learned

Exercise 1 Read the following paragraphs. Indicate which paragraphs are well organized and which are not by circling the appropriate word (*good* or *bad*) at the end of each paragraph. Refer to the outline of a well-organized paragraph in the preceding section.

a. (1) Athletics is an important part of life on most American campuses. (2) In addition to required physical education courses, voluntary programs are provided for health, recreation, and the development of teams for intercollegiate competition. (3) Most coeducational schools belong to an athletic league. (4) The teams within the league play against one another, aiming for the league championship. (5) Football is the college sport that stirs up the most national interest. (6) At large schools, promoting football, developing a team, and playing before huge crowds have become a big business. (7) Season tickets are sold for substantial prices. (8) Games, complete with student marching bands and entertainment, are large productions. (9) Other sports—particularly basketball, swimming, and track—are also pursued with enthusiasm. (10) Some schools also have competitive tennis, skiing, sailing, wrestling, soccer, and baseball. (11) Indeed, sports play a significant role in American college life.[3]

good   *bad*

---

[2]Adapted from Tiersky and Tiersky, *Customs and Institutions: A Survey of American Culture and Traditions*, p. 157.

[3]Adapted from Tiersky and Tiersky, *Customs and Institutions: A Survey of American Culture and Traditions*, p. 158.

b. (1) The schools of a particular society or country usually pass along the accepted customs, ideas, and beliefs of that society. (2) Through the years, schools have had several important aims. (3) These include (a) acquisition of knowledge, (b) intellectual discipline, (c) education for citizenship, (d) individual development, (e) vocational training, and (f) character education.[4]

good   bad

c. (1) When a person's behavior changes, he has learned something. (2) He may learn outside of school as well as in school. (3) A child may learn words and sentences so that he can communicate with others. (4) A person may learn to walk, to run, to jump, or to handle tools and operate a machine. (5) He may learn attitudes of liking and disliking and loving or hating. (6) He may learn facts such as $4 + 4 = 8$, or that the Declaration of Independence was adopted in 1776. (7) He may learn to deal with other persons courteously and fairly or rudely and violently. (8) So no matter what he learns, the process involves changing behavior.[5]

good   bad

d. (1) One of the purposes of education is the development of the individual. (2) The development of any well-rounded person calls for attention to his or her physical, social, and emotional life, as well as to his or her intellectual growth. (3) Healthful recreation, artistic appreciation, and the ability to express oneself in the arts are important for self-development. (4) The acquisition of knowledge is another function of education. (5) Schools have always insisted that students acquire the knowledge, information, and skills that are important for an educated person. (6) Students are taught to read and write one or more languages, to use a system of numbers, and to acquire knowledge of such subjects as history, literature, and science.[6]

good   bad

Exercise 2   For each "bad" paragraph you identified above (you should have found two), indicate which part was missing (the topic sentence, the bridge, examples, or the return), and supply it in the space provided on the next page.

---

[4]Adapted from *World Book Encyclopedia* (Chicago: Field Enterprises Educational Corp., 1962), pp. 56–58.

[5]Adapted from *World Book Encyclopedia.*

[6]Adapted from *World Book Encyclopedia.*

Paragraph number: _____

Missing part: _____

Added sentence(s): _____

_____

_____

_____

Paragraph number: _____

Missing part: _____

Added sentence(s): _____

_____

_____

_____

Exercise 3 In Bernard's English class yesterday, the teacher led a discussion on differences in education around the world. As the class talked, one student recorded the ideas on the board. The students seemed very interested in the issue of competition at large U.S. universities because the situation is so different in their home countries. Today Bernard's teacher has assigned a paragraph based on yesterday's discussion. Here are the notes that appeared on the board:

- Students very competitive at large U.S. universities.
- Professors have many tricks to prevent cheating.
- High failure rate at large American universities.
- Exam questions switched at the last minute.
- Professors supply test booklets; students cannot use their own.
- Monitors patrol large exam halls.
- Students sit far away from each other.
- Cheating is a cause for dismissal from most U.S. universities.
- At large U.S. universities, you rarely see students comparing grades, sharing notes, or forming study groups, especially at the undergraduate level.
- A certain percentage of undergraduates is systematically eliminated from popular majors by extremely difficult introductory courses.

Do the same as Bernard did: Look at the notes and write a well-organized paragraph with all the necessary elements (topic sentence, bridge, examples, and restatement). Since the notes suggest more than one main idea, you must choose a unifying theme for your paragraph and eliminate all unrelated ideas. Feel free to add information based on your knowledge and experience. First, complete the chart to help you organize your ideas.

Topic Sentence: _____

_____

_____

Bridge: _____

_____

_____

Example 1: _____

_____

_____

Example 2: _____

_____

_____

Example 3: _____

_____

_____

(Example 4:) _____

_____

_____

Restatement: _____

_____

_____

Exercise 4 Marta's English class had a similar activity. The class discussed the purpose of higher education. Some students thought the purpose of education is for personal enrichment and growth. Others, including Marta, believed that the only reason to pursue higher education is to prepare for a profession. Here are Marta's notes from the discussion. Read them carefully and follow the same procedure as you did for Bernard's assignment in Exercise 3. You can choose to write about one side of the issue or the other, or both sides. Again, it may be necessary to add information.

Marta's notes:

- A college education, regardless of one's major, trains one to think; it disciplines the mind.
- Studying Latin may not be career oriented, but it disciplines the mind and improves memory.
- Students learn general skills in college that can be applied to any profession.
- There is a great deal of competition for good jobs in the real world; you should prepare for this with a good educational background in a chosen field.
- Students who do not prepare for a career while in college are wasting time and money.
- Focusing on a career while in college is a waste of time because it is impossible to predict the future job market and economy.
- Psychology courses can be useful in everything from childrearing to business management.
- You can study languages, literature, and music in your free time, *after* you've gotten a good job.
- An economics major is more likely to get a good job after graduation than an art history major.

Topic Sentence: _____

_____

_____

Bridge: _____

_____

_____

Example 1: _____

_____

_____

Example 2: _____

_____

_____

Example 3: _____

_____

_____

(Example 4:) _____

_____

_____

_____

_____

Assignments

1. Write a unified, well-organized paragraph in which you show the advantages or disadvantages of one of the following issues in education:

   - small classes versus large ones
   - majoring in the humanities versus majoring in science
   - pursuing an education for professional training versus pursuing a career for self-fulfillment
   - cooperation versus competition among students
   - college professors as authority figures versus college professors as consultants

   (You may also discuss an issue not mentioned here.)

2. Write a paragraph in which you compare a school or college in your country with one in the United States or Canada.

3. React to, agree with, or disagree with the following quotation: "An educated person has more advantages than an uneducated person."

PART FOUR

EVALUATING FOR REWRITING

Working with Your Partner

Exchange the paragraph(s) you wrote with a partner and answer the following questions.

1. Underline the topic sentence. Does it have all of the characteristics for a good topic sentence discussed in Chapter 1?

   Yes _____   No _____

2. Read the rest of the paragraph. Does each sentence relate to and develop the topic sentence?

   Yes _____   No _____

If the answer is *no*, find the irrelevant sentences and cross them out. Is the paragraph more unified now? You may need to add new, relevant ideas to develop the topic sentence further.

3. Put a star next to the explanatory (bridge) sentence. Does it help you understand the main idea?

Yes _____   No_____

Why? Why not? _____

_____

4. How many examples are there? List them briefly here:

_____

_____

_____

_____

_____

5. Is there a restatement of the main idea in the last sentence?

Yes _____   No_____

Is the language of the topic sentence paraphrased?

Yes _____   No_____

6. Now rate the paragraph, keeping in mind all the material you've learned in this chapter as well as in the previous chapter.

Rating	The Paragraph . . .
1	needs rewriting.
2	is good, but there are some unclear sentences.
3	is very good; it's clear and there are no missing parts (topic sentence, bridge, examples, restatement).

Working on Your Own

Now you should be ready to evaluate your own paper. Go through the questions again. Take into consideration what your partner said about your paper when he or she evaluated it. Are there missing parts? Is there more to add? Words to change? Finally, score your own paragraph before you turn it in to the teacher. Did you earn a 3?

CHAPTER 3
THE FAMILY

1.

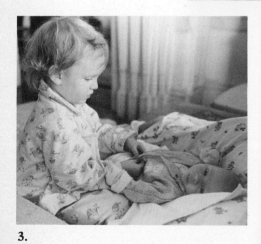

2.

3.

4.

PART ONE

IDEAS FOR WRITING

THE FAMILY IN TRANSITION

How important a role does the family play in the development of a person's attitudes and behavior? Think for a moment about your own family. How have your parents or brothers or sisters helped you become who you are today? What role have other family members—such as aunts, uncles, and grandparents—played? Look closely at the photos of American families on page 52. Study the positions, facial expressions, and body language of the family members. Try to interpret the roles of the family members and their relationships and feelings based on your interpretation of the photos. Discuss the photos with one or two classmates and then work together to complete the following chart. What can you say about

Photo 1: _____

_____

_____

Photo 2: _____

_____

_____

Photo 3: _____

_____

_____

Photo 4: _____

_____

_____

Brainstorming

Write the new words you learned from your classmates to describe the roles, relationships, and feelings of the family members in the photos.

Roles	Relationships	Feelings
_____	_____	_____
_____	_____	_____
_____	_____	_____
_____	_____	_____

General Terms

_____

_____

_____

Freewriting

Write for ten minutes without stopping about your family. Describe your relationships with family members.

Reading for Ideas

Masao is a foreign student doing research on the American family. His assignment is to interview an American about his or her family to learn about the roles, relationships, and feelings among family members. He chooses to interview Alice, a professional woman in her mid-thirties, who is an acquaintance from the university. He sees her in the student union. Read their conversation.

Prereading Questions

1. How does a person's position in the family (for example, being the oldest, middle, or youngest child) and a person's gender (being male or female) determine his or her relationship with parents and siblings?
2. How active a role should fathers play in raising children?

Masao: Excuse me, Alice. Would you mind if I asked you a few questions about your family? It's an assignment for one of my classes.
Alice: Okay. I have a couple of minutes. Go right ahead.
Masao: Thanks. Let's see . . . tell me about your family when you were a child.

Alice: Well, there were five children—four girls and one boy. I'm the oldest. I always felt that because I was the oldest, I got the most attention from my parents.

Masao: How did you get along with your brothers and sisters?

Alice: Actually, I hardly knew my brother because he was the youngest. I was closest to Linda, who's a year younger. The middle sisters were close to each other, and we didn't do much together.

Masao: What were your parents like?

Alice: Dad was rarely home because he worked so hard, so Mom took care of the kids. The only time we saw Dad was when there was a crisis or when someone had misbehaved.

Masao: What was your parents' relationship like?

Alice: They got along pretty well; they ate dinner together every night in front of the t.v. after we had gone to bed. I wasn't aware of much then. But I do know that they met in college and fell in love. When their parents didn't permit them to marry, they eloped. They ran off and got married anyway.

Masao: How romantic! How about now, Alice? Do you get together with your family often?

Alice: I see them only on holidays. We don't have much in common anymore. I don't like my sisters' husbands, and my brother is from a different generation.

Masao: What about your parents?

Alice: I'm not sure how they're getting along, but Dad seems to be helping out around the house more now that we all have moved out. Mom's much happier now that she's working.

Masao: That's really interesting. Your family is very different from mine. You've helped me a lot, Alice. Now I have lots of information for my assignment.

Alice: Great! If you need any more information, give me a call.

Postreading Questions

1. What would Alice and her brother be likely to disagree about?

   _____

   _____

2. Why do you think Alice's mother is happier now that she is working?

   _____

   _____

3. Why do you think Alice doesn't like her sisters' husbands?

   _____

   _____

4. What does Alice's father do more around the house now?

_____

_____

5. How do you think Alice's parents feel about Alice?

_____

_____

6. Are there any similarities between Alice's relationships with her brother, sisters, and parents, and your relationship with your family members?

_____

7. Do your parents have the same roles that Alice's parents have?

_____

8. Review Alice's feelings about each member of her family. Are your feelings about your family members similar or different?

_____

9. Predict the future for Alice, her parents, and her brother and sisters based on what you know from the interview.

_____

_____

_____

Gathering Information

Interview an American about his or her family. Ask questions that give you information about family roles, relationships, and feelings. You will use this information as the basis for a writing assignment later in the chapter. Ask about both past and present experiences. Take notes. Use the interview between Masao and Alice to give you ideas. Write the questions you will ask in the following space.

Interview Questions:

_____

_____

_____

_____

_____

PART TWO

LANGUAGE FOR WRITING

DESCRIBING ROLES, RELATIONSHIPS, AND FEELINGS

The following chart illustrates the language one can use to describe Alice's roles and relationships within and feelings about her family. Study the italicized words and phrases and how they are used in each sentence. Then think about how you relate to your family members and how your close friends feel about their brothers, sisters, and parents. Complete the chart by adding as many new words and phrases as possible to describe the people you select. You will think of new words by describing relationships that are different from Alice's. If you cannot think of new words and phrases by describing the roles, relationships, and feelings of friends or family members, consult a dictionary or thesaurus for synonyms and antonyms.

Name	Roles	Relationships	Feelings
Example:			
Alice	She is:	She is:	She is:
	the *eldest.*	*distant from* her brother.	*aloof from* her family.
	the *big sister.*	*close to* her sister.	She feels *different from* the others.
	a *role model for her brother* and sisters.	*independent from* her parents.	*She feels that* family ties are not *important.*

(continued on next page)

Name	Roles	Relationships	Feelings

Exchange your chart with a classmate and discuss each other's examples, making notes on new words and phrases. Write the new words and phrases in the following space.

Practicing What You've Learned

1. Write a paragraph about Alice's family. Focus on the feelings she has about her brother, sisters, and parents. Use the vocabulary you've learned in this section.

2. Write a paragraph about your family. Choose either roles, relationships, or feelings as the focus of your paragraph. Use the following space to chart or outline your ideas. Then write a topic sentence that captures the essence of these ideas.

———————————————————————

———————————————————————

———————————————————————

———————————————————————

———————————————————————

———————————————————————

———————————————————————

PART THREE

SYSTEMS FOR WRITING

PARAGRAPH COHERENCE: PRONOUNS AND PARAPHRASING

As you have seen in Chapters 1 and 2, a paragraph must develop one main idea. This idea is presented in the topic sentence, and the rest of the paragraph explains, illustrates, and restates the idea. In addition, the sentences in a paragraph must move smoothly from one to the other. This is called *coherence.* If you look up the word *coherence* in the dictionary, you will find that it means "logical or natural connection." Writers attempt to establish a logical and natural connection between sentences. They can do this by using:

■ pronouns that refer to nouns already mentioned:

Although *Alice's father* was living at home and considered himself an active parent, he didn't know his children well. *He* saw them only on weekends and holidays.

■ restatements of words or expressions from a previous sentence; this is called a *paraphrase:*

He saw them only on *weekends and holidays.* He preferred seeing them only on *his days off* because he didn't have much patience for the varying moods and constant demands of small children.

Practicing What You've Learned

Exercise 1 In the following paragraphs the noun has been repeated. Rewrite each paragraph, making the sentences more coherent by substituting pronouns instead of nouns. Hint: Be careful not to overuse pronouns. It is appropriate to repeat the subject every three or four sentences and to use pronouns elsewhere, depending on the length of the sentences. Your reader should not have to question who or what the pronoun refers to.

> **a.** A new breed of women, called "supermoms," is becoming abundant. Supermoms are women who work while raising families. The typical supermom assumes a major role in managing her family. The typical supermom makes day-care and preschool arrangements as well as organizing after-school events. The typical supermom keeps the house clean and well stocked with food. The typical supermom also has a position of responsibility at her place of work. The typical supermom is often required to spend long hours and make important decisions at work. In addition to these responsibilities, the typical supermom manages to see her friends occasionally, play tennis, and take courses at the local community college. Although the work load she takes seems insurmountable, the typical supermom handles it well.

> **b.** To many American families, the family pet is as important as the other members. The family pet lives indoors, eats special pet food, and is often taken on family outings and vacations. The family pet receives toys on holidays and special medical care when necessary. When the family pet dies, it is often buried in a pet cemetery. American pets are truly honored members of the family.

Exercise 2 To paraphrase, you must be able to use synonymous words and phrases for repeated ideas. Practice paraphrasing by providing synonymous expressions in the right column.

	Paraphrase
brothers, sisters, parents	_____
get along with someone	_____
be close to someone	_____
elope	_____
get together with someone	_____
have something in common with someone	_____

Exercise 3 Now incorporate paraphrases into the following paragraph to reduce repetition and to make it more coherent. Try to vary the paraphrase for the same expression.

c. In the Middle East, families are the most important social units, and, in general, these families are very close. These families are close because they get together often and family members usually get along well with each other. First of all, families from the Middle East often live together or live in the same region. As a result, brothers, sisters, and parents get together often. Brothers, sisters, and parents get together on the weekends and on holidays. In addition, Middle Eastern families are often large, and the members usually get along well with each other. Female family members get along well with each other because their roles are similar and they have a lot in common. The children get along particularly well with their grandparents. Male family members get along well with each other, too, because they share responsibility for making major family decisions. Middle Eastern family members learn early the importance of the family and develop an allegiance to it through their close relationship with family members.

PARAGRAPH COHERENCE: TRANSITION WORDS AND EXPRESSIONS

Transition words and expressions are important coherence devices because they tie sentences together and show relationships between ideas. Look at the following sentences:

1. There has been an increase in the number of people who live alone.
2. As a matter of fact, one in five Americans lives alone.
3. In the past, most women started families in their twenties.
4. Nowadays, however, many women are having first babies in their mid- and late thirties.

Notice that both Sentences 1 and 2 are about the topic of living alone. The transition *as a matter of fact* connects the two sentences and establishes a relation between the ideas. It indicates that Sentence 2 further supports Sentence 1 by providing (in this case) a specific statistic. *As a matter of fact* always introduces further support, but in addition to statistics, it can introduce a specific example, event, or detail.

Similarly, Sentences 3 and 4 are about the same topic: at what age women have babies. The transition *however* connects the sentences by indicating that the idea in Sentence 4 is opposite, different, or contrasting to the idea in Sentence 3. Study the following chart that lists some useful transitions and the relationship they establish between sentences.

Transitions	Functions
However On the other hand Conversely	Show the other side/a contrasting point
Similarly In addition Furthermore Moreover Besides	Introduce a new/additional idea that supports the previous sentence
For example In fact	Expand a point by providing a specific illustration or application
Thus Therefore In conclusion	Conclude a point by providing a result; may relate to two or three previous sentences

Because these transitions occur between sentences, they are called *sentence connectors*. These sentence connectors usually come at the beginning of a sentence and are followed by a comma.

Practicing What You've Learned

Exercise 1   Use the sentence connectors from the chart above in the following pairs of sentences. First determine the relationship between ideas in the two sentences. This will show you the function of the necessary transition. Then add an appropriate transition word or expression by rewriting the second sentence of each pair. Remember to include necessary punctuation.

Example:

a. Alice, like many American young adults, does not see her parents often.

b. Masao, from Japan, lives with his parents and shares much of his life with them.

Relationship: *Ideas in Sentence "b" contrast to those in "a".*

New Sentence b: *On the other hand, Masao, from Japan, lives with his parents and shares much of his life with them.*

1a. American family members are taught to respect independence and individuality.

1b. It is not unusual to see grown siblings who have very different lifestyles and have extremely different philosophies about life.

Relationship: _____

New Sentence **1b:** _____

_____

_____

_____

2a. Couples can choose to get married in a traditional religious ceremony, in a personalized, less formal celebration, or simply in a court.

2b. In most states, if they are at least eighteen, they can get married without parental consent.

Relationship: _____

New Sentence **2b:** _____

_____

_____

_____

3a. Parents of American teenagers who misbehave have a variety of effective forms of punishment.

3b. Being grounded is particularly unpleasant for teens because they are not permitted to leave home or meet their friends.

Relationship: _____

New Sentence **3b:** _____

_____

_____

_____

4a. Most young people from countries where marriages are arranged believe that marriages based on love are best.

4b. Some old people believe that arranged marriages are ultimately more satisfying to the partners and more successful.

Relationship: _____

New Sentence **4b:** _____

_____

_____

_____

5a. As divorces increase, custody laws, which always left children with their mothers, are changing.

5b. Now it is not uncommon for fathers to receive full custody of their children.

Relationship: _____

New Sentence **5b:** _____

_____

_____

_____

Exercise 2 The following paragraph discusses how people in various cultures choose mates. Complete the paragraph by providing appropriate sentence connectors in the spaces provided.

The degree of freedom in choosing a mate varies from culture to culture. In North America, it is not uncommon for a young man and young woman to meet, fall in love, and marry almost without the knowledge of their family members.

_____, 1 they are not completely free. In most states, they must obtain a license and go through a simple ceremony, and in some states they are forbidden to marry if

they are first cousins. _____, 2 in other cultures there is much less choice and much more control by family

members. _____, 3 marriages arranged by heads of families are very common outside North America.

_____, 4 until recently, most Chinese brides and grooms did not even see each other before their wedding.

_____, 5 whether family members select marital partners depends on the culture one comes from.[1]

Note that although sentence connectors are almost always used to link sentences together, they may also occur in the middle or

---

[1]Adapted from Queen and Habenstein, "Cultural Variations in the Family," in *The Family in Various Cultures* (Belmont, Calif.: Wadsworth Publishing Co.), 1975.

at the end of a sentence. For example, in the third sentence of the paragraph above, *however* could occur at the end of the sentence. And in the fifth sentence, *however* could occur after "In other cultures" or at the end. Experiment with the placement of *however* in completing your assignments for this chapter.

Exercise 3   Read the following paragraph carefully. All coherence devices (sentence connectors, paraphrases, and pronouns) are missing. In the spaces at the end of the paragraph, give as many appropriate words and expressions as possible for each item. Make sure that your choices maintain the ideas of the paragraph. When you are finished, exchange papers with a classmate and compare your answers.

   If there is one word that characterizes the American family within the last fifty years, it's change. There used to be mainly

two types of _____: 1 the extended and the nuclear. The

_____ 2 most often included the mother, father, children, and some other relatives, such as the grandmother and grandfather,

living in the same house or nearby. _____, 3 aunts, uncles,

cousins, nieces, and nephews were all living _____ 4 and were

able to lend a helping hand. _____ 5 as job patterns changed and the economy progressed from agricultural to industrial, people were forced to move to different parts of the country for

job opportunities. _____ 6 moves split up the extended

family. _____, 7 the nuclear family became more prevalent.

_____ 8 consisted of only parents and the children. Now, besides these two types of traditional groupings, the word *family* is being extended to include a variety of other living arrangements.

1. _____

2. _____

3. _____

4. _____

5. _____

6. _____

7. _____

8. _____

Assignments

1. Write a paragraph based on the interview you did in Part One. Focus on roles, relationships, and/or feelings. Use the vocabulary and expressions you have learned in this chapter.

2. Write a paragraph in which you compare one aspect of family life in your culture to that of American culture. For example, you may choose to discuss the role of the father in raising children, the role of grandparents, the responsibility of male/female children, loyalty to the family, or how couples meet.

3. Write a paragraph including facts about the typical family in your home country or city today. Use at least eight of the following verbs in your paragraph.

to consist of	to live (with)	to be	to become
to marry	to prefer	to have	to work
to do	to take care of	to like	to get along with

4. It is the year 2000. You are reporting on a typical family in America or in your country during the 1980s. Write a paragraph using information from any of the sections in this chapter.

5. It is 1950. You are a gifted social scientist who is making predictions about the future of the family. Write a paragraph about a typical family in America or in your country as it will be in the 1980s.

PART FOUR

EVALUATING FOR REWRITING

These exercises are designed to help you revise and improve the paragraphs you wrote for the assignment in Part Three. First, answer the questions about a classmate's paper that your teacher chooses. Then, exchange your own paper with a classmate and answer the questions about his or her paragraph. Finally, answer the questions about your own paragraph.

Working with the Class

1. Underline the sentence that contains the main idea.

   a. Is this the first sentence?   Yes _____   No _____

   b. Is there an explanation?   Yes _____   No _____

c. Is there at least one example?　　　Yes _____　No _____

d. Is there a restatement of the
　 main idea?　　　　　　　　　　 Yes _____　No _____

If the answers to all of the questions above are *yes*, go on to Question 2. If not, revise the paragraph so that each of the answers is *yes*.

2. Are there any sentences that do not relate to the main idea? If a sentence does not relate, omit it.

3. Now look at how the sentences are linked to each other. Look for examples of coherence devices.

　 a. Put a dotted line (. . . . . .) under pronouns that refer to nouns already mentioned.

　 b. Put a broken line (_ _ _ _) under paraphrases.

　 c. Put a straight line (_____) under transition words.

　 d. How many coherence devices did you find? _____

　 e. For each coherence device, has the writer used it correctly? Does it link sentences together?　　Yes _____　　No _____

If the answer to *e* is *no*, the writer should revise the paragraph by adding coherence devices, changing them, or rewriting sentences.

Working with Your Partner

Exchange papers with a classmate and answer Questions 1 through 3 from "Working with the Class" for your partner's paper. Where possible, give suggestions for revision and improvement based on what you've learned in the previous chapters.

Working on Your Own

Finally, evaluate your own paper by answering the same questions as objectively as possible. Rewrite your paragraph and incorporate revisions suggested by the questions.

CHAPTER 4
HEALTH

1.

2.

3.

4.

5.

6.

PART ONE

IDEAS FOR WRITING

HEALTH AND EVERYDAY LIVING

A person's health is affected by many things: diet, work, weather, leisure-time activities, and mental attitude. This chapter explores issues in health and how they affect people in both positive and negative ways. Can you think of how your health is affected by your diet? Your work? The weather? Your hobbies? Your attitudes and moods? Discuss the answers to these questions with a classmate.

Look closely at the photos and answer the questions that follow.

1. What health problems do you think the man shown in the top left photos has? Why?

2. Why are the commuters in Photo 3 upset? How does a hurried lifestyle affect one's health? Describe the photo of the man commuting by bicycle.

3. In what ways does the type of work a person does affect his or her physical and mental well-being?

4. Can you identify with any of the people in the photographs? That is, can you find similarities between what they are doing and what you do?

Brainstorming

Look at the photos and, in small groups, talk about the causes of good health and poor health. Discuss physical and mental health and go as deeply into the topic as possible. As you talk, keep notes in the following chart on the words and expressions that you use. An example is done for you.

Photo	Effect	(WHY?)	Cause 1	(WHY?)	Cause 2
1.	overweight		overeats		doesn't exercise
2.					
3.					

Photo	Effect		Cause 1		Cause 2
		(WHY?)		(WHY?)	

4. _____

_____

5. _____

_____

6. _____

_____

7. _____

_____

Freewriting

Choose one of the photos at the beginning of the chapter and write for ten minutes without stopping on why this person looks/is the way she or he is.

Reading for Ideas

Prereading Questions:
What Kind of Person Are You?

To prepare for the following reading entitled "Type A Behavior and Type B Solutions," take this quiz and discuss your answers with the class. Then read the article.

1. Do you have a strong desire to excel in your studies?   Yes _____ No _____

2. Do you have a fear of being dependent on others?   Yes _____ No _____

3. Do you feel a need to control others?   Yes _____ No _____

4. Do you prefer to be continually *doing* things rather than *thinking* about things?   Yes _____ No _____

5. Are you disinterested in anything
   that does not relate directly to
   your studies/work?   Yes ____   No ____

6. Is making a great deal of money
   important to you?   Yes ____   No ____

7. Are you often physically tense?   Yes ____   No ____

8. Are you always in a hurry?   Yes ____   No ____

9. Do you drink a lot of coffee?   Yes ____   No ____

10. Do you make a list of tasks to be
    accomplished each day?   Yes ____   No ____

"Type A Behavior and Type B Solutions"

America's ambitious and competitive culture teaches destructive
thought and behavior patterns that increase the risk of heart disease.
The problem is not only with men; women share it too. However, most
Type A's are men. New research suggests that Type A's can increase
5 both the quantity and quality of their lives if they try to change their
behavior patterns.

Type A behavior is characterized by time pressure, interpersonal
hostility, and great ambitions for social and economic success. It is
based on a strong desire to excel, deep insecurity, a fear of
10 dependence, a need to control others, and an insatiable urge for
accomplishment. Type A men prefer to act rather than to think and
tend to neglect all aspects of life that do not directly relate to their
work. Ex-Secretary of State Alexander Haig has been classified as
a typical Type A.

15 A recent study demonstrated that men could substantially improve
cardiac health by modifying Type A behavior. This finding is significant
because about 75 percent of the male population in urban areas
exhibit Type A behavior, as well as more than 90 percent of all patients
with coronary heart disease.

20 These men can change their lives with the help of monthly groups
led by psychologists, psychiatrists, and cardiologists and by making
changes on their own. Philosopher-writer Sam Keen has been
changing his own life in these ways for almost twenty years. "I
suppose I was an early Type A," Keen remembers. "I realized I was
25 completely obsessed by my work. It was helpful for me to realize that
my Type A behavior was a serious problem. In fact, it is the dominant
way of being for middle-class, white, American men."

Keen's self-directed program for change involved the reversal of three behavior patterns that are deeply rooted in the culture of the ambitious American male: goal orientation, money orientation, and time pressure. [30]

"The Type A man has an engineer's view of the world," Keen explains. "We become so involved in our work, so busy drawing blueprints of our dreams, that we cut ourselves off from much of the real joy and richness of life. We build our careers into great, powerful [35] engines, but may end up ignoring signs that we're on the wrong track. And we tend to experience any unexpected or non-work-related happening as a roadblock to our success.

"But many of life's joys come from the unexpected. The world is capable of giving many gifts and blessings. Type A men miss all that [40] because they're just not paying attention.

"One of the Type B skills is learning to catch the moment. Yesterday, for instance, I was out for a walk and came across a patch of really extraordinary golden-orange flowers. I picked a handful and put them in a vase on my windowsill. I find my eyes wandering back [45] to them again and again. They feed me. They reassure me. They delight me. I didn't plan that—I just saw the flowers and picked them. Twenty years ago I would never have noticed them. The only contact I had with flowers was as something on my "To Do" list.

"When we talk about Type A behavior," Keen continues, "we're [50] not just talking about ideas running through people's heads. Type A men have abnormally tense muscles, hold their stomachs drawn in, and keep their chests inflated, exactly the kind of posture apes use in trying to scare off their rivals. They do everything to stimulate that state: drink coffee, eat sugar, smoke cigarettes, and sometimes [55] snort cocaine. Type A men always wear watches, and they're always in a hurry. They are obsessed with time.

"Type A's feel that it's a dog-eat-dog world, and if you don't have a million bucks in the bank, something horrible may happen to you. The Type B solution is to ask yourself, 'What do I really *want* to be [60] doing in the world, and what does the world *need* me to do?' All too frequently the Type A man follows the dollar sign and never takes the opportunity to find out what he really wants in life.

"Some Type A's are afraid to change because they think they will have to give up the rewards of their intense work involvement. Actually [65] just the opposite is true—I enjoy my work more than ever before. Your goal becomes doing the *right* work, not just more of the work you happen to be doing. I'm fond of the term *vocation,* because it has the sense of being *called* to do something. To find your true vocation, you must search for your deepest sense of what's important, [70] what gives you joy, and what uses your special gifts. Ask yourself, 'If I didn't have to worry about money, what is the work I would do for free?'

75 "The reason I decided to make some changes was that I woke up one day and realized that all the behavior patterns that had brought me to a certain measure of success had also crippled my ability to be available to the world. I had accomplished much of what I wanted, but in doing it I had bought into a life of constant hassles and had accumulated some pretty formidable defenses. I decided to take it 80 as my task to slowly let go of those hassles and begin to step out from behind those defenses.

"How have I changed? My friends say I've really relaxed. I think I'm finally kinder to myself, kinder to other people. My pace is slower. I certainly know a lot less than I used to. Life seems richer. I'm happier 85 than ever in my work. And I certainly am having a better time."

Adapted from Sam Keen, *Medical Self-Care* (Spring 1983): 36–41 (in conversation with Tom Ferguson, M.D.).

Postreading Questions

1. According to the article, what causes Type A behavior?

_____

_____

_____

2. What are some of the results of Type A behavior? Think of health conditions.

_____

_____

_____

_____

3. Give some examples of people that you know (friends, family, or well-known people) who exhibit Type A behavior.

_____

_____

_____

_____

4. Is it possible to change Type A behavior? _____

5. What are the three behavior patterns of the ambitious Type A American male? Give specific examples of each of these behavior patterns.

_____

_____

_____

_____

_____

_____

6. Is there evidence of Type A or Type B behavior patterns in your culture? Do they exist among men, women, or both? To what extent?

_____

_____

_____

7. Can you explain why Type A behavior is characteristically American?

_____

_____

_____

Gathering Information

Find out to what extent the average American is concerned about his or her health. Interview at least five Americans by asking these questions:

1. How big a role does health play in your day-to-day life?

$$1 \quad\quad 2 \quad\quad 3 \quad\quad 4 \quad\quad 5$$
a big role $\longrightarrow$ a small role

2. What are some things you do on a daily basis to stay healthy?

3. How important is health to you compared with other life goals? First, think of your goals, then rank order them in descending order of importance. Possible goals: financial independence, a successful career, a high position at work, the ability to travel throughout the world, a home, a happy marriage, a large family,

_____ , _____ ,

_____ , . . .

The most important should come first.

PART TWO

LANGUAGE FOR WRITING

SHOWING CAUSES AND EFFECTS

Look at the following chart. On the left are some common health conditions, and on the right are causes for these conditions. Match each health condition with its appropriate cause. Some conditions may have more than one correct cause. The first one is done for you. When you finish, discuss your answers with the class.

Causes ————————————————————————→ **Effects**

Causes	Effects
Type B behavior	excess weight
a good diet	a long life
overeating	heart disease
exercise	strong muscles
Type A behavior	hypertension
smoking	normal blood pressure
relaxing	lung cancer
stress	a healthy heart

Here is a list of expressions used to discuss causes and effects. Study the list carefully and notice how each of the expressions is used. Notice the difference between *causes* and *leads to*.

One (the) cause of . . . (noun) is . . . (noun).
. . . (noun) leads to . . . (noun).
            results in
            results from
            causes
            has an effect on
As a result of . . . (noun), . . .
As a result, . . . (sentence connector: the cause appears in the previous sentence).
Because ⎫
Since   ⎬ + clause, . . .
Because of . . . (noun), . . .
The (one) effect (result) of . . . (noun) is that. . . .

Practicing What You've Learned

Show the relationship between the causes and effects in the chart by using one of the expressions from the list. Underline the expression. The first one is done for you.

Example: *A good diet <u>results in</u> a long life.*

1. _____

2. _____

3. _____

4. _____

5. _____

6. _____

7. _____

EXPRESSING POSSIBILITY AND PROBABILITY

When talking about causes and effects, you often will find it necessary to *qualify* your statements with words that express *possibility* and *probability* (*can, could, may, might*) unless you are 100-percent certain of what you are concluding. A 100-percent degree of certainty is usually the result of a scientific study. You can express causes and effects that are *likely* to be true based on casual observation, as long as you qualify your statements with words such as *can, could, may,* and *might*. Study the following pairs of sentences.

1a. Obsession with work and making a lot of money *may* lead to health problems among American males.

1b. Obsession with work and making a lot of money leads to health problems among American males.

2a. Drinking coffee, eating sugar, and smoking cigarettes *might* cause heart disease.

2b. Drinking coffee, eating sugar, and smoking cigarettes cause heart disease.

3a. Hypertension *could* be the result of Type A behavior.

3b. Hypertension is the result of Type A behavior.

4a. Good mental and physical health *can* be the result of exercise and a well-balanced diet.

4b. Good mental and physical health is the result of exercise and a well-balanced diet.

What is the difference in meaning between the first and second sentences of each pair? What do each of the italicized words mean? What is the function of the italicized words?

Practicing What You've Learned

Exercise 1   The following paragraphs, taken from a newsletter, discuss the danger of hypertension for both adults and children. The words that express possibility and probability are missing. Read the paragraphs and fill in the blanks with *can, could, may,* or *might.*

Hypertension

High blood pressure places a severe strain on the heart, blood vessels, and kidneys. That strain _____ eventually cause the heart to enlarge and become thickened. In some cases, the heart _____ fail. High blood pressure _____ also cause your blood vessels to "overstretch," weaken, or burst; a ruptured blood vessel in the brain _____ cause a stroke or even paralysis. The third, very serious complication related to high blood pressure is kidney failure. When the kidneys cease to function, they no longer filter out waste products. The result of kidney failure _____ be serious illness, even death.
  Adults are not the only victims of high blood pressure. Children, too, _____ have high blood pressure. Like adults, children won't usually have any symptoms to warn them. If symptoms do occur, it _____ not be until after serious problems already have occurred. A growing child's normal blood pressure _____ fluctuate even more than an adult's, particularly during puberty, so one or two high readings are not necessarily cause for alarm. In order for your physician to interpret your child's blood pressure accurately, he or she might have to use several readings.

79

Exercise 2   Write sentences about what *can, could, may,* or *might* happen to these people as a result of their behavior.

1. Masao smokes too much.

   _____

   _____

   _____

2. Alice doesn't get very much exercise.

   _____

   _____

   _____

3. Karen skips meals.

   _____

   _____

   _____

4. Dave is obsessed with his work and has little time for recreation.

   _____

   _____

   _____

5. Marta consumes more calories than she burns up each day.

   _____

   _____

   _____

6. Gloria exercises for an hour each day and doesn't drink coffee or smoke cigarettes.

   _____

   _____

   _____

7. Eric is very nervous and is under a lot of stress at school.

   _____

   _____

   _____

   _____

8. Nick never eats junk food.

_____

_____

_____

PART THREE

SYSTEMS FOR WRITING

PARAGRAPH DEVELOPMENT

In Chapters 1, 2, and 3 you learned that a well-developed paragraph contains a complete topic sentence that is well organized, that gives the reader an idea of what the paragraph is about, and that includes sentences that flow from one to the other. In this chapter you are going to learn how to develop a paragraph by using different types of support and by deepening your discussion of the main idea.

Types of Supporting Material

In addition to using examples to develop the topic sentence of a paragraph, you can use facts, statistics, and anecdotes. As you saw in Chapter 2, an _example_ is a person, a quality, or an event taken from a number of things of the same kind to show the common quality of the rest or to illustrate a general rule.

Type A men are obsessed with their work and tend to discount aspects of life that do not relate to their work. _Alexander Haig is a typical Type A._

A _fact_ is an idea that is true or an event that has happened.

Men in a recent study conducted by Meyer Friedman changed their lives with the help of monthly groups led by psychologists, psychiatrists, and cardiologists.

A _detail_ is a small part of a fact. It is also a true idea or an event that happened.

A _statistic_ is a number, often part of a collection of numbers, that represents facts or measurements.

About 75 percent of men in major urban areas exhibit Type A behavior. More than 90 percent of all patients with coronary heart disease are Type A's.

An *anecdote* is a short story about a particular person or event that can be used to illustrate a point. Anecdotes are not used as often in academic writing as examples, facts, and statistics.

One skill associated with Type B behavior is appreciating and maximizing spontaneity. Sam Keen, trying to learn Type B behavior, is gradually learning to be spontaneous. He was proud of himself one afternoon recently. *He was taking a walk and spotted a patch of bright golden-orange flowers. Struck by their beauty, he stopped among them, enjoying the sight and smells. After pausing to enjoy them, he picked a handful of them and has put them in a vase on his window sill.* He enjoys looking at them and remembering how he allowed himself to stop and enjoy the moment.

Now go back to the reading "Type A Behavior and Type B Solutions" and locate further examples, facts, statistics, and anecdotes. Count the number of each type of support and record it below. How many did you find?

Examples _____ Facts _____ Statistics _____ Anecdotes _____

It is important to use sufficient support when you develop a paragraph. You may use just one type of support or several types. The test of whether the main point of a paragraph has been sufficiently supported and adequately developed is if the reader is not left with any questions about the aspect of the topic you've chosen to develop.

Deepening the Discussion

It is important to satisfy your reader by fully developing a paragraph. You want to explain your main idea and support it with examples, facts, statistics, or anecdotes. Read the following paragraph about medical treatment for Navaho Indians.

a. (1) The Navaho medicine man is remarkable in that he is both priest and doctor at the same time. (2) Each of his chants and ceremonies requires so much in the way of knowledge, specific equipment, and the exact memorization of sand paintings that a single medicine man learns only a few ceremonies thoroughly in his lifetime. (3) "Blessingway," a two-day ceremony, is the foundation of the whole ceremonial system. (4) There are three major divisions of the system: "Holyway," "Evilway," and "Lifeway." (5) In these three categories there are about twenty-six distinct ceremonial parts.

Although the paragraph introduces the reader to some interesting facts, it leaves many questions. The paragraph needs further development. An effective way to *deepen the discussion* in any paragraph and to develop it further is to ask and answer a question at the end of each sentence. Notice how this is done in the following chart.

Number	Sentence	Question
(1)	The Navaho medicine man is remarkable in that he is both priest and doctor at the same time.	How?
(2)	Each of his chants and ceremonies requires so much in the way of knowledge, specific equipment, and the exact memorization of sand paintings that a single medicine man learns only a few ceremonies thoroughly in his lifetime.	How much?
(3)	"Blessingway," a two-day ceremony, is the foundation of the whole ceremonial system.	How? Why?
(4)	There are three major divisions of the system: "Holyway," "Evilway," and "Lifeway."	What are they?
(5)	In these three categories there are about twenty-six distinct ceremonial parts.	Does the last sentence restate the first sentence?

Now reread the paragraph and notice how the answers to the questions have provided further development.

b. The Navaho medicine man is remarkable in that he is both priest and doctor at the same time. In the old days he was the only person of the tribe who performed religious ceremonies. These were chants and ceremonies that are still performed today to help people recover from illness and accident. Each of these chants and ceremonies requires so much in the way of knowledge, specific equipment, and the exact memorization of sand paintings that a single medicine man learns only a few thoroughly in his lifetime. The amount of knowledge required has been compared to that expected of a modern graduate student for a master's degree. "Blessingway," a two-day ceremony, is the cornerstone of the whole ceremonial system. It lends its prayers and myths to all the other chants and controls the meaning and purpose of the whole. Stemming from "Blessingway" are three major divisions of the system: "Holyway" chants attract the good powers to cure illness; "Evilway" banishes the effects of evil things such as witches or ghosts; "Lifeway" is specific for physical injuries and accidents. In these categories there are about twenty-six distinct ceremonial parts.[1]

Practicing What You've Learned

Exercise 1   In the following exercise you have been given the "bare bones" of a paragraph. Each sentence is followed by a question. Rewrite and develop the paragraph by incorporating the answers to the questions into the new paragraph.

High blood pressure is harmful to one's health. (How?) It affects the heart. (How?) It also affects the blood vessels. (How?) The third complication of high blood pressure is that it contributes to kidney failure. (How?)

Hint: Refer to the exercise on hypertension in Part Two. You may want to rewrite complete sentences to make your new paragraph more coherent.

Exercise 2   Now develop the following "bare-bones" paragraphs by *asking* and *answering* questions at the end of each sentence. Refer to Part One of this chapter and your own knowledge and experience to add supporting examples. Exchange papers with a classmate when you are finished.

Nick is very conscious of his health. He eats the proper foods. He exercises regularly. Finally, he has a positive mental attitude.

Eric is under a lot of stress at school. He is very nervous. He is disorganized, and he tends to put things off to the last minute.

PARAGRAPH ORGANIZATION

You have seen one way to develop your paragraphs. Here is some information on organizing them. A paragraph written to describe

---

[1]Adapted from David S. Sobel, *Ways of Health: Holistic Approaches to Ancient and Contemporary Medicine* (New York: Harcourt Brace Jovanovich, 1979), p. 49.

causes and effects can be organized in several ways. The writer can announce the result(s) and then list the cause(s) or describe the cause(s) first and then the result(s). In some cases, an idea can be both a result and a cause. Read the following paragraphs. On the lines next to each of the paragraphs indicate whether the numbered sentences describe causes (C) or results (R) or both (B).

1 _R_   **a.** (1) The Hunzukuts, who live eighteen miles from Russia's southern border at the northern tip of Pakistan,
2 _____   are said to be the healthiest people in the world. (2) Their foods are pure and natural, and commercial fertilizers
3 _____   are forbidden by law. (3) No insecticides, no artificial
4 _____   additives of any sort are permitted. (4) This helps create crops that promote health and prolong life.

1 _____   **b.** (1) In a land called Hunza, where six mountain ranges meet in awesome silence and peaks reach up to twenty
2 _____   thousand feet, men and women live to be over ninety. (2) Even when they are advanced in years, the Hunzukuts
3 _____   are able to do the work of much younger people. (3) They do not suffer from diseases such as mumps, measles, or
4 _____   chicken pox. (4) They do not have high blood pressure,
5 _____   heart disease, arteriosclerosis, or cancer. (5) They enjoy
6 _____   peace of mind and lead stress-free lives. (6) All of this is a result of natural living and natural health foods and genetics.

1 _____   **c.** (1) Nowadays, many chemicals are added to foods. (2)
2 _____   Astringents, solvents, and emulsifiers, common food additives, drain vitamins and minerals from the blood-
3 _____   stream and tissues and can cause premature aging. (3) Other food additives used to preserve food inhibit the
4 _____   beneficial functions of nutrients in food. (4) Finally, bleaching agents cause digestion problems.

Exchange papers with a classmate and compare patterns of organization. You should have these answers:

a. R C C C   **b.** R R R R R C   **c.** C R R R or C B B B

Was one pattern more *dramatic* than the others? Was one pattern easier to understand?

As a writer, you choose a pattern or organization according to what you want to emphasize. For example, if you have causes to discuss, you may want to put them first. Or, if the result is more important, you may want to put it first. Finally, if you want to emphasize both causes and results, you may want to use the following pattern: C C C R R R.

Practicing What You've Learned

Now practice these patterns of organization by writing a paragraph on each of the following topics. Use the pattern of organization indicated.

Organization Pattern	Topic
a	Heart disease (as a result)
b	A healthy body (as a result)
c	Television and health (as a cause)
You choose	Overeating (as a cause)
You choose	Exercise (as a cause)

Assignments

1. Write a paragraph about causes and effects of good health. Use the interviews you conducted from Part One to support your topic sentence.

2. Write about the causes and effects of poor health. Again, use your interviews for support.

3. Argue for or against a particular remedy for an illness or health condition. Develop support for your argument by explaining what your remedy does or doesn't cause.

4. Discuss advantages or disadvantages to a particular health care system.

5. Agree or disagree with the following quote: "An apple a day keeps the doctor away."

PART FOUR

EVALUATING FOR REWRITING

Working with Your Partner

Exchange papers with your classmate and answer the following questions about his or her paragraph.

1. How many types of support can you find? Write each type that you find.

_____

_____

_____

_____

_____

_____

2. Does the support the writer uses help develop the main idea? If the answer is _no,_ offer suggestions for changing or adding more or different types of support. If the answer is _yes,_ go on to the next question.

_____

_____

_____

_____

_____

3. Has the writer developed the paragraph adequately? That is, were you, as reader, left with any questions about the main idea of the paragraph?

Yes _____   No _____

If your answer is _yes,_ write the sentence(s) that could be more fully explained.

_____

_____

_____

_____

_____

4. Now look at how the writer has organized the paragraph. If the paragraph discusses causes and effects, show the pattern of organization.

_____

_____

_____

_____

Is this an effective pattern of organization? That is, does it make the relationship between causes and effects clear?

Yes _____   No _____

5. Underline all the cause-and-effect expressions. How many did you underline? _____ To the best of your knowledge, are they used correctly?

Yes _____   No _____

6. Do you have any other general comments about this paragraph?

_____

_____

_____

_____

_____

7. Now reread the paragraph to make sure the sentences are linked together smoothly. Is the paragraph coherent?

Yes _____   No _____

8. Now rate the paragraph, keeping in mind all that you've learned in this chapter as well as in previous chapters.

Rating	The paragraph . . .
1	needs rewriting.
2	is good, but there are some unclear sentences.
3	is very good; it is clear and sufficiently supported.

Working on Your Own

After evaluating your partner's paper, you should be ready to evaluate your own work with some objectivity. Go through the questions again. Take into consideration what your partner said about your paragraph when he or she evaluated it. Is there more to add? Are there words to change? Can you clear up any language mistakes? Finally, score your own paper before you turn it in to the teacher. Rewrite the paragraph until you can give it a 3!

CHAPTER 5
MONEY MATTERS

New York Stock Exchange.

PART ONE

IDEAS FOR WRITING

THE SUCCESSFUL ENTREPRENEUR

What is your definition of "success"? To some people, being successful means achieving happiness in your personal life. To others, it means having your own business, earning a lot of money, and having a great deal of responsibility and power within an organization. Can you think of some people who have had this second kind of success? To what do they owe their success? Luck? Hard work? Superior intelligence? The following information is about a person who has had great success in the business world. Study his photo and resume and the revenues (earnings) chart of one of his companies. Then answer the questions that follow.

1. What is Porter Hurt's current occupation? _____

2. Describe Porter Hurt's employment history from 1961 to the present.

   _____

   _____

   _____

   _____

   _____

3. Is Porter Hurt a successful person? Why?

   _____

   _____

   _____

4. Do you think his transition over sixteen years from sheetrock installer to president of three successful companies is unusual? Why or why not?

   _____

   _____

   _____

   _____

   _____

5. Generally, is it easy for a person to go from being a worker to a company executive? Can you think of some other people who have done this?

_____

_____

6. Is PH Components a successful company? How do you know?

_____

_____

_____

Porter Hurt.

RESUME

Porter Hurt
PH Components
35920 Santa Rosa Avenue
San Jose, CA 95101

Experience

1980-present	**President**, Actrix Computer Corporation, San Jose, CA. Manufacturer of portable computers. Annual revenues: $1 million.
1978-present	**President**, Testology Inc., San Jose, CA. Circuit board sales. Annual revenues: $1.5 million.
1975-present	**President**, PH Components, San Jose, CA. Distribution of electronic parts. Annual revenues: $1.5 million.
1967-1975	**Stockboy and Sales Manager**, Kierulff Electronics, San Jose, CA. Was promoted to Sales Manager after one year; was made General Sales Manager in 1975.
1961-1967	**Sheetrock Installer**, O'Brien Construction, San Jose, CA.

Education   High school diploma, 1959.

Personal   Married; two children. Excellent
            health.

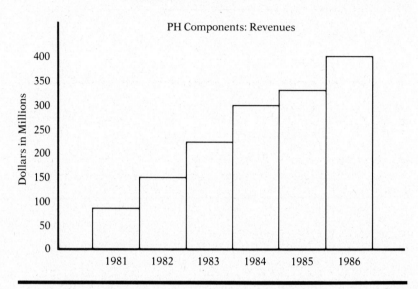

Brainstorming

In small groups, look again at Porter Hurt's photo, resume, and the revenues chart for his company, PH Components. In the following chart, write all the words and expressions you can think of to describe his personal qualities, his various occupations, and the company.

Personal Qualities	Occupations	PH Components
Examples:		
lucky	worker	successful
ambitious	executive	profitable
_____	_____	_____
_____	_____	_____
_____	_____	_____
_____	_____	_____

Personal Qualities	Occupations	PH Components
_____	_____	_____
_____	_____	_____
_____	_____	_____
_____	_____	_____

Freewriting

Write for ten minutes without stopping and describe the personal qualities of a successful business person. It can be someone you know or a famous person that you know about.

Reading for Ideas

The following story about Porter Hurt is adapted from an article in the business section of a newspaper. Answer these questions before you read.

Prereading Questions

1. What skills are necessary to be a good poker player?
2. Are these skills similar to those required for success in the business world?
3. What is a "millionaire"?
4. Where is Silicon Valley? What is it known for?

An Off-the-Wall Success Story:
Porter Hurt's Amazing Rise from
Sheetrocker to High-Tech Millionaire

Sixteen years ago, Porter Hurt drove four thousand nails a day into four tons of sheetrock working as a laborer in Silicon Valley.

Today Hurt drives a specially designed Cadillac limousine around the valley, where he owns and serves as president of three electronics
5 companies that he predicts will have revenues of $300 million next year.

Hurt is hardly a typical high-tech entrepreneur. He never went to college and has no training in electronics and little understanding of computers, even though one of his companies manufactures them. "I know it's hard to understand, but the whole fairy tale is true," says the forty-two-year-old Hurt during a conversation in his modest San Jose (California) office.   10

This is truly a "rags-to-riches" story. Hurt financed his entry into the electronics industry with an original source of capital: his weekly poker winnings. Tired of working as a sheetrocker and envious of the lifestyle described by his poker-playing partners who worked in   15
the electronics industry, Hurt talked his way into a job as an electronics distributor. He took a pay cut of almost $1,000 a month in May 1967 to work as a stockboy at Kierulff Electronics' Palo Alto office. "My rent was $395 a month, so I played poker ten to twelve hours every Wednesday and Friday night to support my family," Hurt   20
recalls.

Called a natural salesman by some of his associates, Hurt quickly moved up the ladder at Kierulff. Within four years he became sales manager, and by the time he was thirty-five years old he was general sales manager and given an annual salary of $60,000. "It was a   25
skyrocket situation, but he had that salesman's ability of dealing with people," said Fred Snider, Hurt's first boss at Kierulff. "He could fall into a hole and strike oil—he's got luck and seems to be in the right place at the right time," Snider says.

Despite rapid success, Hurt had a strong desire to have his own   30
business and in 1975, he left Kierulff to start his own electronics distributing company, PH Components.

Hurt started his business from his home, using the family car to deliver parts to his customers. As his company grew, Hurt started assembling printed circuit boards, an important part of thousands   35
of electronic products. Noting a real need in the industry, he started a second company, named Testology, in 1978.

Testology was very successful because it allowed electronics manufacturers to get all their circuit board parts from one place. Before Testology was founded, manufacturers had to go to as many   40
as eighty different places for printed circuit board parts, then have them assembled and tested. Testology did all of this and gave the customers an unheard-of, one-year guarantee on the circuit boards. Today, Testology supplies circuit boards to all the major computer manufacturers in Silicon Valley.   45

Around this time, Ted Pollard, president of Actrix Computer Corporation, came to Hurt for capital and Testology's help in building computers. During one meeting, Hurt asked Pollard for majority ownership of Actrix. "Pollard threw me out of his office," Hurt says.

50 But Pollard eventually called him back. Today Hurt owns 82 percent of Actrix stock and serves as president of the company.

Hurt was not at all unsure about heading Actrix, even though he knew almost nothing about computers. "My being a novice at computers has been an advantage for the company," Hurt says. "If 55 our engineers can't get me to understand what they're doing, then I know the public won't understand the product and won't buy it."

Hurt says Actrix will ship twenty thousand computers this year. He predicts that revenue will jump to an $80 million annual rate by next year. Although some stock market analysts say Actrix will have a 60 difficult time competing in the already overcrowded computer market, his longtime acquaintances are sure of his success. "Porter has a unique capability and the desire and the ambition to succeed as an entrepreneur," says Vic Gerano, a director at Four-Phase Systems, Inc., who has bought parts from him since 1971.

65 Despite his success, Hurt says he has not changed his work habits. "I bought a new house, some cars, and a $150,000 speedboat, but I haven't taken a vacation in years and I still work eighty hours a week," he says.

Sometimes he longs for the simpler life of a sheetrocker. "I think 70 I slept better then because the mental fatigue is a lot worse than the physical," he says. "I wouldn't trade places, however!"

John Eckhouse,
San Francisco Examiner, September 11, 1983

Postreading Questions

1. Why did Porter Hurt quit his job as a sheetrocker?

_____

_____

2. Was his transition from stockboy to general sales manager at Kierulff considered unusually quick by his first boss, Fred Snider? Explain.

_____

_____

_____

3. Why was Testology so successful?

_____

_____

4. Go back to the article and find the explanation of how Hurt became majority owner and president of Actrix Computers. What adjectives can you use to describe the personality of someone who behaves the way Hurt did in this situation?

_____

_____

5. Why was Porter Hurt so successful? Locate information in the article to support your answer.

_____

_____

_____

6. According to Porter Hurt, why is his lack of knowledge about computers *not* a problem? Do you agree with him?

_____

_____

_____

7. Do you think Porter Hurt is happy? Find evidence for your opinion in the article, if there is any.

_____

_____

_____

8. What are the material symbols of Porter Hurt's success?

_____

_____

_____

_____

9. Would you like to do what Porter Hurt has done? Could you?

_____

_____

_____

10. Can you think of people in your country who have similar stories?

_____

_____

11. Hurt says, "I haven't taken a vacation in years and I still work eighty hours a week." Do you think Hurt is telling the truth? Is he complaining? Is he proud of himself? Is he a Type A or Type B personality? (Refer to Chapter 4.) What words can you use to describe someone with work habits like Hurt's?

   _____

   _____

   _____

   _____

   _____

12. The following is a list of idiomatic expressions used in the article. Do you know what they mean? Locate them in the article. Then study their contexts (the words and sentences around them) and guess what each one means. Write your guesses here, then check with your teacher to see if you are correct.

Idiom	Meaning
to talk one's way into something	_____
	_____
to have a knack for something	_____
	_____
to trade places	_____
	_____
a skyrocket situation	_____
	_____
to deal with people	_____
	_____

Gathering Information

The following people are Americans who achieved great success in business. Choose one name from the list and find out as much as you can about the person and the business(es) he or she created. Go to the library and use the following sources of information. Take notes on the information you gather and organize the notes in a summary that you will share with your teacher and classmates.

- the reference librarian, a good person to start with
- the card catalog, especially if the business person is no longer alive
- the *Reader's Guide to Periodical Literature*, a general index, especially good for people who are still living
- the *Business Periodicals Index*, an index to business publications, good for people who are still living

1. Ray Kroc (1902–1984)
   President
   McDonald Corporation

2. Kyupin Philip Hwang (1936–)
   President
   Televideo Corporation

3. A. P. Giannini (1870–1949)
   Founder
   Bank of America

4. Levi Strauss (1829–1902)
   Founder
   Levi Strauss & Co.

5. Mary Wells Lawrence (1928–)
   President
   Wells, Rich, Greene, Inc.

6. C. J. Walker (1867–1919)
   Inventor, Entrepreneur
   Cosmetics

PART TWO

LANGUAGE FOR WRITING

DESCRIBING SUCCESSFUL PEOPLE

Listed below are some words and expressions that are useful in describing different aspects of business from the article "An Off-the-Wall Success Story." Find each word and expression in the article and study its meaning in the context of Porter Hurt's story.

Business Terms

WORDS	IDIOMATIC EXPRESSIONS
revenues	to move up the ladder
capital	to be in the right place at the right time
to finance	a natural salesman/woman
financing	a rags-to-riches story
high tech	to head up a company
entrepreneur	
entrepreneurial	

Adjectives that describe successful people are also going to be useful in this chapter. Working with one or two partners, make a list of adjectives that describe people who are successful in business. As you make your list, consider Porter Hurt, the people you gathered information on in Part One, and other successful people you know.

Person	Quality (Adjective)
Example:	
Porter Hurt	lucky
	ambitious
_____	_____
_____	_____
_____	_____
_____	_____
_____	_____
_____	_____
_____	_____
_____	_____
_____	_____

Practicing What You've Learned

Now use each word and expression in an original sentence about a successful business person that you know of or the person that you gathered information on in the previous section. You can write about Porter Hurt if your sentences are quite different from those in the article.

TURNING ADJECTIVES INTO ABSTRACT NOUNS

When you want to emphasize a quality that a person has, use the noun form of an adjective that describes him or her. See how the focus shifts in the two sentences below:

a. Porter Hurt was successful in business because he was *lucky.*

b. *Luck* is one of the factors that led to Porter Hurt's success.

Luck and other similar nouns are called *abstract nouns.* They are *uncountable;* that is, they cannot be preceded by *a/an* and they have no plural form. Abstract nouns represent *concepts,* whereas concrete nouns such as *book* and *table* represent objects you can see and touch.

Sentences with abstract nouns such as Sentence **b** are more formal than sentences containing the adjective counterpart of the abstract noun.

Practicing What You've Learned

Exercise 1 For each adjective you listed in the preceding chart, supply the abstract noun form in the following chart.

Adjective	Abstract Noun
Example:	
lucky	luck
ambitious	ambition

Exercise 2 Now write five sentences about five successful businesspeople using the abstract nouns from the exercise you just did.

_____

_____

_____

_____

_____

_____

_____

_____

_____

_____

_____

PART THREE

SYSTEMS FOR WRITING

UNITY AND COHERENCE
THROUGH KEY WORDS AND CONCEPTS

As you saw in Chapters 2 and 3, _unity_ and _coherence_ are important features of good paragraphs. In this chapter, you are going to see how carefully chosen words and expressions that are repeated and paraphrased throughout a paragraph help maintain unity and coherence. These words and expressions are called _key words_ or _key concepts_.

Writers establish key concepts in a topic sentence and recall them through repetition and paraphrasing throughout the paragraph to maintain coherence and unity. This helps the reader follow the ideas expressed in the paragraph. See if you can recognize the key concept in the following topic sentence:

> The success of many entrepreneurs is often attributed to their ability to find a need in the marketplace and fill it.

The key concepts are _success of many entrepreneurs_ and _find a need and fill it_. In other words, you expect to read in this paragraph about how entrepreneurs become successful by finding out what is missing in the marketplace and producing it. Furthermore, you probably expect the writer to give you some examples of people who have done this. To fulfill your expectations, the writer will have to mention these ideas again and again in the paragraph, but not necessarily in the same words used in the topic sentence.

Although it is acceptable to recall key concepts using the same words and expressions you use in the topic sentence, it is much better to use synonymous words and phrases to avoid repetition. Synonymous words and phrases make the paragraph livelier and more interesting to the reader. Read the following paragraph and answer the questions.

(1) A willingness to take risks is one of the most important qualities that lead to success in business. (2) A person who is willing to take risks is one who, despite the possibility of failure, will charge ahead in a new business venture with confidence in his or her abilities. (3) For example, Porter Hurt, president of PH Components, was taking a great risk when he decided to leave his job as a sheetrock installer for a lower-paying one in the electronics industry. (4) He knew that there was a future in this field, and he was confident in his ability to rise quickly to the top. (5) As a result, he is today the president of not one, but three electronics companies that will have revenues of $300 million next year. (6) Because he was willing to take a chance, Porter Hurt went from blue-collar worker to millionaire in sixteen years.

1. What two key concepts are contained in the topic sentence? Write them in the following chart.

2. Are these concepts repeated throughout the paragraph? That is, do most of the sentences contain words or phrases that are similar in meaning to the expressions you listed in Question 1?

In the chart, list the words or expressions that recall at least one of the key concepts in the topic sentence.

Sentence   Key Concepts

1   _____   _____

Words and Expressions That Recall Key Concepts

2   _____   _____

_____   _____

3   _____   _____

_____   _____

4   _____   _____

_____   _____

5   _____   _____

_____   _____

6   _____   _____

_____   _____

3. Look at the words and expressions you listed in Question 2. Are they (a) *identical to* the expressions you listed in Question 1, or are they (b) *synonyms or paraphrases* of the key concepts? Or are they a combination of (a) and (b)?

4. What is the *purpose* of this repetition and paraphrasing of key concepts throughout the paragraph?

_____

_____

Practicing What You've Learned

Exercise 1   In the paragraphs below, the key concepts in the topic sentences have been circled. Read each paragraph carefully, find the words and expressions that recall the key words, and underline them.

   a. (Public accounting) consists largely of (auditing and tax services.) An _audit_ is a review of the financial records of an organization. Auditing is usually performed at fixed intervals of time—perhaps quarterly, semiannually, or annually. And as the tax laws have grown increasingly complex, not only corporations but also individuals have had to utilize the services of accountants in preparing their tax forms. Businesses, government agencies, and nonprofit organizations all employ public accountants either regularly or on a part-time basis.[1]

   b. (Leading executives) in the the best-run U.S. companies share the quality of being able not only to establish (strong corporate values,) but also to live according to those values. These leaders have the ability to transmit the essential qualities of their companies to other people. We describe that sort of leadership as a "value-driven style." A good example of this type of top executive is J. Willard Marriott, Sr., founder of the Marriott Corporation, who was still reading every single complaint card

---

[1]Adapted from Sandra Costinett, *The Language of Accounting in English* (New York: Regents Publishing Company, 1977), pp. 5–6.

that came into that lodging and restaurant company until he was over eighty years old.[2]

Exercise 2   Read the following paragraphs carefully. Locate the key concepts in the topic sentences and circle them. Then identify the words and expressions that recall the key concepts by underlining them.

a. Nations use the capital of other nations to build their industrial bases. This capital is used to build factories and develop mines, among other things. For example, the railroads of the United States and South America were built by British capital. This capital paid for the costs of construction, including materials and the wages of the workers, and the locomotives and freight cars. More recently, American, Japanese, and European corporations have provided funds to explore for oil and to build new automobile, steel, and chemical plants around the world.[3]

b. Shaklee Corporation is one of the most successful companies in San Francisco because the managers understand the importance of giving both within and outside the corporation. It is successful because top-level management cares about the welfare of their employees as well as the community in which they do business. Their employees have access to free fruit-juice bars and the use of the company's indoor health facility with its 8,000-square-foot track and cardiovascular clinic. Once a year the headquarters close for the day so employees can spend it at Golden Gate Park participating in athletic events. Shaklee Corporation gives to the community as well. They sponsored the

[2]Adapted from "Well-Run Companies: The Secret of Success," an interview with Thomas Peters (coauthor of *In Search of Excellence*), *U.S. News and World Report* (October 10, 1983), pp. 74–75.

[3]Adapted from Peter K. Oppenheim, *The Language of International Finance in English: Money and Banking* (New York: Regents Publishing Company, 1976), p. 7.

Adopt-an-Animal program at the San Francisco Zoo. They helped keep the Golden Gate Park Band alive by sponsoring the musicians for one month of the year and enlisting eleven other companies as monthly sponsors.[4]

Exercise 3 The following is a topic sentence with the key concept(s) underlined. Write a paragraph that supports it by using synonymous words and phrases wherever possible to recall the key concept in the topic sentence. Underline your synonymous key words and phrases when you have finished.

A person who <u>achieves success in business</u> in a short amount of time is usually <u>hard working</u> and <u>highly motivated</u>.

Assignments

Write a paragraph on one of the following topics. Use new vocabulary and expressions you learned in this chapter and make sure that your main idea is recalled by synonymous key words and expressions. Develop your ideas by using information from the research you did in Part One.

1. Describe a successful entrepreneur and focus on his or her approach to business.

2. What is one personal quality that leads to success in the business world? Why? Use the information you gathered in Part One to support your main idea.

3. Choose a successful company and discuss the main factor that has led to its success.

4. "Being a novice at computers has been an advantage for the company," according to Porter Hurt. "If our engineers can't get me to understand what they're doing, then I know the public won't understand the product and won't buy it." Discuss the advantages or disadvantages of a company executive having technical knowledge of his or her product.

5. Explain, agree, or disagree with the following quote: "Success in business depends more on *who* you know than on *what* you know."

---

[4]Adapted from "Executive Comment," *San Francisco Business* (San Francisco Chamber of Commerce: September 1983).

PART FOUR

EVALUATING FOR REWRITING

Working with Your Partner

Exchange the paragraph(s) you wrote with your partner and answer the following questions.

1. Underline the topic sentence. What are the key concepts?

    a. _____

    b. _____

    c. _____

2. Are the key concepts generally recalled throughout the paragraph?

    Yes _____   No _____

3. By writing the key word or expression in the following blanks, give a sentence-by-sentence analysis of how paragraph continuity is maintained throughout the paragraph. Also, indicate where unity and coherence are lacking, if necessary.

    Sentence   Key Concepts

    1   _____   _____

    Words and Expressions That Recall Key Concepts

    2   _____   _____

    3   _____   _____

    4   _____   _____

    5   _____   _____

    6   _____   _____

    7   _____   _____

    8   _____   _____

    9   _____   _____

    10   _____   _____

4. Study the words and expressions you listed. How many of them are exact repetitions of the language used in the topic sentence?

    _____ How many are paraphrases? _____

    If there is too much repetition, supply acceptable synonymous words and phrases:

Original Word/Expression	Paraphrase	PART FOUR
_____	_____	
_____	_____	
_____	_____	
_____	_____	
_____	_____	

5. Now rate the paragraph, keeping in mind all the material you've learned in this chapter as well as in previous chapters.

Rating	The paragraph . . .
1	needs rewriting.
2	is good, but there are some unclear parts.
3	is very good; it's clear and the ideas are sufficiently developed.

Working on Your Own

Now you should be ready to evaluate your own paper. Go through the questions again. Take into consideration what your partner said about your paper when he or she evaluated it. Is there more to add? Words to change? Finally, score your own paragraph before you turn it in to the teacher. Did you earn a 3?

CHAPTER 6
LEISURE TIME

PART ONE

IDEAS FOR WRITING

LEISURE-TIME ACTIVITIES

How often do you have free time? What do you like to do? Do you spend your free time alone or with others? Look at the following photos, which show people doing different things in their leisure time. Study the photos, then answer the questions with a partner.

1. How are the people in the photos using their leisure time?

2. Which of the activities do you enjoy?

3. Which of the activities do people in your country do in their leisure time?

4. Which of the activities are passive? Which are active?

5. Which activities are done with other people? Which are done alone?

6. Which activities are done at home? Which are done away from home?

7. Which activities require training and which do not?

8. Which cost money and which do not?

9. Which are educational and which are entertaining?

Brainstorming

1. Look at the photos again. Then list the activities that you and your partner described in the space below. The first one is done for you.

Activities

watching t.v.

_____

2. Now look at the photos and your list, and think of characteristic features that describe at least two of the activities. We'll call these *categories*. Refer to the questions above, but think of additional categories also. Write the categories below. One has been done for you.

Categories

passive

_____

_____

_____

_____

3. Finally, complete the chart by listing the categories in the boxes and writing the corresponding activities in the spaces below each box. Some of the activities may fall into more than one category.

watching t.v.
sleeping
listening to music
reading

Freewriting

Write for fifteen minutes without stopping about your favorite lesiure-time activity. Why do you prefer it to other activities? Does it require special skill? Do you do it with others or alone?

Reading for Ideas

Prereading Questions

1. What are the Olympic Games?
2. How often do they occur?
3. When and where will the next Olympic Games take place?
4. What are some of the events?
5. What events have athletes from your country participated in? In which events have athletes from your country been particularly successful?
6. Which are your favorite Olympic events? Why?
7. As you read the article, note the organization of ideas in the passage. What two main categories of information does it contain? What examples describe each category?

The Olympic Games

Every four years, amateur athletes from nations all over the world compete in an athletic exhibition called the Olympic Games. The Olympic Games include many different types of sports events. They take place in a different host nation each time and they are begun with a runner who carries a blazing torch into the arena to light the Olympic flame. Olympic events are divided into summer and winter games. The summer Olympics run for about two weeks, and the winter Olympics last ten days.

There are many types of Olympic events. The summer events are subdivided into five areas: track and field sports, gymnasium competition, water sports, team events, and riding competitions. The winter Olympics are always held in a mountainous country where there is plenty of snow. The slopes and snow are necessary for the winter events, which are categorized as follows: skiing, ice-skating, and team sports. Skiers compete in four kinds of events: jumping events, downhill and cross-country races, and the slalom. Skating

events are subdivided into speed skating and figure skating. Finally, team sports include ice hockey and bobsledding events. There are two types of bobsledding events, where either two- or four-person
20   teams race their sleds over icy courses.

People all over the world look forward to the summer and winter Olympic games every four years because of their international appeal and because of the wide variety of sports events.

Adapted from *The World Book Encyclopedia* (Chicago: Field Enterprises Educational Corp., 1961), pp. 567–68.

Postreading Questions

1. Organize the information in the selection on the Olympic Games by filling in the organizational chart on page 116. As you can see, boxes have been provided for the two *main* divisions in the article and for all the supporting ideas that go with the two main parts. See how many boxes you can fill in without looking back at the reading selection.

2. Look up any new words from the selection and write their meanings.

    _____

    _____

    _____

    _____

    _____

3. Now, reread the passage and underline the words and expressions that are used to show how the information is *categorized*. Write the expressions below. The first one is done for you.

    a. *are divided into* _____

    b. _____

    c. _____

    _____

    _____

Discuss these questions with two or three classmates:

4. Have you ever attended the Olympic Games? Where and when?

    _____

115

The Olympic Games

I. [ ]

    A. [ ]

    B. [ ]

    C. [ ]

    D. [ ]

    E. [ ]

I. [ ]

    A. [ ]

        1. [ ]

        2. [ ]

        3. [ ]

        4. [ ]

    B. [ ]

        1. [ ]

        2. [ ]

    C. [ ]

        1. [ ]

        2. [ ]

5. When were the last summer Olympics? Winter Olympics? Where did they take place?

_____

_____

6. Are the Olympics important to sports fans in your country? Has your country ever hosted the Olympics?

_____

7. Can you think of any Olympic champions from either your country or another?

_____

Gathering Information

Leisure time in the United States and Canada is highly valued. How do your American friends and acquaintances spend their leisure time? Ask two Americans how they spend their leisure time and why they prefer this leisure-time activity. Arrange your information in a chart like the following one. When you finish, share your information with the class.

Informant	Age	Sex	Occupation	Activity	Reason Activity Is Enjoyed
_____	_____	_____	_____	_____	_____
_____	_____	_____	_____	_____	_____
_____	_____	_____	_____	_____	_____
_____	_____	_____	_____	_____	_____
_____	_____	_____	_____	_____	_____
_____	_____	_____	_____	_____	_____
_____	_____	_____	_____	_____	_____
_____	_____	_____	_____	_____	_____

PART TWO
LANGUAGE FOR WRITING
CLASSIFYING LEISURE-TIME ACTIVITIES

Often in academic and scientific writing, students are required to organize information into groups or classes. Study the following expressions, which are useful in classifying information. Note the underlined word endings.

Leisure-Time Activities:

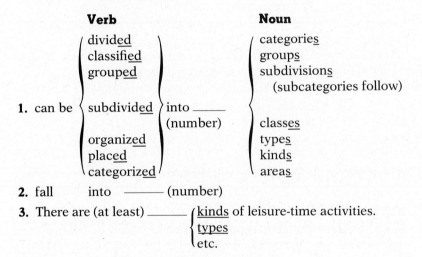

Verb		Noun
divid**ed**		categorie**s**
classifi**ed**		group**s**
group**ed**		subdivision**s**
		(subcategories follow)
1. can be subdivid**ed**	into ——	
	(number)	class**es**
organiz**ed**		type**s**
plac**ed**		kind**s**
categoriz**ed**		area**s**

2. fall   into ——— (number)

3. There are (at least) ——— { kind**s** of leisure-time activities.
type**s**
etc. }

Practicing What You've Learned

Exercise 1 Refer to the article on the Olympic Games in Part One. Write sentences about further subdivisions of the summer Olympic events by using the expressions in the chart. Study the following example before you begin.

Track and field sports
  races
  jumping
  decathalon

Water sports
  swimming
  rowing
  yachting

Gymnasium competition
  fencing
  gymnastics
  weight lifting

Riding competition
  horsemanship
  cycling

Example: Water sports in the summer Olympics can be divided into three areas: swimming, rowing, and yachting.

Exercise 2 A study was done recently at Nick's college about how students spend their free time. The most popular categories of free-time activities follow. Using the expressions in the chart on page 118, write a sentence for each category. Subdivide the general category into classes based on your knowledge and experience. Study the example.

Categories

Museums	Vehicles used for recreation
Television programs	Music[1]
Reading materials[1]	Movies
Sports	Food[1]
Vacations	

Example: Museums can be *divided* into three types: art, natural history, and anthropology.
(**Or:** There are at least three types of museums: art, natural history, and anthropology.)

PART THREE

SYSTEMS FOR WRITING

PARAGRAPH DEVELOPMENT: GENERAL TO SPECIFIC INFORMATION

Read the following paragraph that Masao wrote about one of his interests, art. As you read, notice the way he organized his ideas. When you finish, work with a partner and answer the questions that follow.

(1) In very broad terms, art is skill in making or doing. (2) There are two types of art: *useful* art—beautiful objects produced for everyday use—and *decorative* art—beautiful objects produced for their own sake. (3) The world's great museums contain many examples of decorative art, such as statuary. (4) Statues, which have been sculpted throughout history to honor important figures as well as all human beings, are made of stone, metal, or other solid material. (5) David, a well-known statue of the

---

[1]Noncount nouns

Biblical hero carved by Michelangelo, was one of the first anatomically accurate sculptures of a human being. (6) It can be seen at the Academy of Fine Arts in Florence, Italy.

Now, answer these questions about Masao's paragraph.

1. What is the topic of the first sentence? _____

   _____

   Is this sentence *general* or *specific*? _____

2. What is the topic of Sentence 6? _____

   _____

   Is it general or specific? _____

3. Now look at Sentences 2 to 5. Decide whether each one is more general or more specific than the sentence that comes before and write your answers below.

   More general or more specific?

   Sentence 2: _____

   Sentence 3: _____

   Sentence 4: _____

   Sentence 5: _____

   Sentence 6: _____

4. Did you find a pattern in Masao's paragraph? Try to draw a picture of it here:

Here's another paragraph that Masao wrote on the subject of art. In what way is it different from the first one?

(1) Art, which is skill in making or doing, can be either useful or decorative. (2) Artists produce beautiful objects for everyday use. (3) For example, chairs and typewriters are designed to perform certain functions, yet they too are sometimes considered works of art. (4) In fact, an Olivetti typewriter is on exhibit at the Museum of Modern Art in New York City. (5) Artists also produce objects for purely decorative purposes. (6) Examples of art for its own sake are sculpture and painting, which are produced solely for the aesthetic enjoyment of the viewer. (7) *Water Lilies*, by Claude Monet, is an example of this type of art. (8) Whether the art object is useful or decorative, its production requires great skill.

Now, answer these questions about Masao's second paragraph.

1. What is the topic of the first sentence? _____

   _____

   How many *parts* does it have? _____

   Are these parts the *same* or *different* in terms of their level of generality? _____

2. What is the topic of Sentence 2? _____

   Is it more general or more specific than Sentence 1? _____

   _____

3. What is the topic of Sentence 5? _____

   How does this sentence relate to Sentence 1? _____

   _____

   _____

4. Now look at Sentences 3, 4, 6, 7, and 8. Describe the relationship of each of these sentences to the ones around it. Consider whether it is more general or more specific.

   Sentence 3: _____

   Sentence 4: _____

   Sentence 6: _____

   Sentence 7: _____

   Sentence 8: _____

5. Did you see a pattern in this paragraph, too? Try to draw a picture of it here:

In order to write a well-developed paragraph that is easy to read, you must support general statements with specific examples. To do this, you must first organize your ideas on the topic according to whether they are general or specific. Here is an example:

> Alice is going to write a paragraph about the Olympic Games. Following are her notes. First, she needs to go through her notes and organize them into categories. Then she needs to determine which ideas are general and which are specific. Try to help her.

Step 1: What's the most general idea in the list? Write a "1" next to it.

Step 2: Find the two major divisions of the most general idea, and write "2" next to them.

Step 3: Finally, decide which category the specific examples fall into. Write "3a" next to the examples that support "summer events" and "3b" next to those that support "winter events."

____2____ summer events

_____ skating events

____1____ the Olympic Games

_____ water sports

____2____ winter events

_____ skiing competition

_____ track and field sports

Here is another list of notes. This time, they're Masao's. Help Masao by organizing them as you did for Alice. Follow the same steps:

Step 1: Write a "1" next to the most general ideas.

Step 2: Write "2" next to the two major divisions of the most general idea.

Step 3: Write a "3a" or "3b" next to the specific examples of each category.

_____ decorative art

_____ Claude Monet's *Water Lilies*

_____ pottery

_____ useful art

_____ **painting**

_____ Japanese *raku* (clay pot)

Did you notice what Alice's and Masao's notes had in common? Both have a general idea with two major subdivisions. The organization looks like this:

1 Topic sentence (most general; has two parts)
   2 First part (more specific)
      3 Fact or illustration related to the first part (very specific)
   2 Second part (same level of specificity as the first part)
      3 Fact or illustration related to the second part (very specific)

Here's another ordering system. Nick is going to write a paragraph about one of the extracurricular activities he enjoys. Read his notes below and arrange them in the order of *general to specific* by numbering the phrases from 1 (most general) to 6 (most specific).

_____ I play the saxophone

_____ music clubs

_____ extracurricular activities at Ohio State

_____ clubs

_____ the jazz band

_____ my solo in next Saturday night's performance

Nick's paragraph would look like this:

1 Topic sentence (most general idea)
   2 More specific information about the topic
      3 More specific information about Sentence 2
         4 More specific information about Sentence 3
            5 More specific information about Sentence 4
               6 More specific information about Sentence 5

So you can either divide your topic into two or more parts and give specific information about the parts, thereby giving specific information about the main idea; or you can take one main idea and go into great depth by giving more and more specific information about that one idea. The pattern you choose depends on what you're writing about. Whichever pattern you choose, the important thing to remember is you must always give clear, relevant, and interesting details and facts to support your general ideas.

Can you think of another general-to-specific paragraph organization pattern that conforms to these guidelines? Here's an example:

1 Topic sentence: two main parts
   2 First part
      3 More specific information about the first part
         4 More specific information about Sentence 3 (etc.)
   2 Second part
      3 More specific information about the second part
         4 More specific information about Sentence 3 (etc.)

Practicing What You've Learned

Exercise 1 Choose either Alice's or Masao's notes and write a paragraph by expanding the notes into sentences. Maintain the order that you established by numbering each sentence. In addition, number the sentences using the same numbers you used in the notes: 1, 2, 3a, 3b. When you've finished, exchange paragraphs with a partner and double-check your ordering.

Exercise 2 Write a short paragraph by expanding Nick's notes into sentences. Maintain the general-to-specific order and number your sentences. You can add a few ideas or elaborate on what Nick noted, if you like. When you finish, exchange paragraphs with a partner and double-check your ordering.

Exercise 3 Now that you have a pretty good idea of how to develop paragraphs by supporting general statements with specific information, take a look at the following paragraphs. The authors had some difficulty with them and need some help in fixing them.

Read each paragraph and try to figure out what is missing. Then rewrite the paragraphs by supplying the missing elements. Number your sentences when you've finished.

a. Many people pursue hobbies in their leisure time. One popular hobby is collecting things. Some people collect useful art objects.

b. Two categories of events in the summer Olympics are track and field events and gymnasium competition. There are many track and field sports. There are also many kinds of gymnasium events.

Assignments

1. In a paragraph, describe the ways in which students at your school spend their leisure time.

2. Write a paragraph about one of the activities you learned about in your interview.

3. Discuss the advantages and disadvantages of the Olympic Games. Consider politics, international cooperation, and so forth.

4. Some people believe that the Olympic Games contribute to international understanding. Do you agree or disagree? Why?

5. Explain, agree, or disagree with one of the following traditional sayings: (a) "Some people live to work; others work to live." (b) "All work and no play makes Jack (Jill) a dull boy (girl)."

PART FOUR

EVALUATING FOR REWRITING

Working with a Partner

Exchange the paragraph(s) you wrote for this chapter with a partner and answer the following questions.

1. Read the first sentence without reading the rest of the paragraph. What organizational pattern do you think it is going to follow?

    a. Top-down   (1

            2

             3

              4

               etc.) _____

b. Divided (1

           2

           3

           2

           3) _____

What is the main idea expressed in this first sentence? _____

_____

_____

2. Now read the rest of the paragraph. Was your answer to Question 1 correct?

Yes _____ No _____

3. Number each sentence in the paragraph to show how each relates to the preceding one.

Was this easy or difficult to do? _____

Why? _____

4. How many "level-3 sentences" (facts and illustrations) did the paragraph have? _____

Briefly list the "level-3 sentences" used in this paragraph:

_____

_____

_____

_____

Were there any level-2 sentences not followed by level-3 sentences? If so, make suggestions for improvement:

_____

_____

_____

_____

5. Were there any level-4 or -5 sentences in this paragraph? What were they? _____

_____

_____

_____

_____

6. Now rate the paragraph, keeping in mind all the material you've learned in this chapter as well as in previous chapters.

Rating	The Paragraph . . .
1	needs rewriting.
2	is good, but there are some elements missing.
3	is very good; it's clear and the ideas are sufficiently developed.

Working on Your Own

Now you should be ready to evaluate your own paper. Go through the questions again. Take into consideration what your partner said about your paper when he or she evaluated it. Is there more to add? Words to change? Finally, score your own paragraph before you turn it in to the teacher. Did you earn a 3?

CHAPTER 7
CREATIVITY

PART ONE

IDEAS FOR WRITING

ARTISTS AT WORK

Creativity is the ability to produce something new and original. Think for a moment of friends and relatives you consider to be creative. Which professions do you think involve creative activities? Now think of some famous people you consider creative. Are they writers? Musicians? Painters? Sculptors? Actors?

Many artists have certain techniques or rituals that help them feel more creative. The photos show various people involved in a creative activity. Study the photos, then answer the questions with a partner.

1. Pable Picasso, painter.

2. Louis Armstrong, jazz musician.

3. Ernest Hemingway, writer.

4. Henry Moore, sculptor.

5. Marcel Marceau, mime.

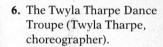

6. The Twyla Tharpe Dance Troupe (Twyla Tharpe, choreographer).

7. Woody Allen, writer, director, actor.

8. Laura Evans, fashion designer.

1. Discuss each of the photos. Which of these personalities are you familiar with? What more do you know about them?

_____

_____

_____

_____

_____

_____

_____
_____
_____
_____
_____
_____

2. Now describe what each of the artists is doing.

_____
_____
_____
_____
_____
_____
_____
_____
_____
_____
_____

3. Look at the surroundings each of the artists has chosen. Do you think an artist's surroundings affect his or her creativity?

_____
_____
_____

Brainstorming

The photos show various artists involved in creative activities. What do you think inspires them? Where do artists get their ideas? With two or three other classmates, make a list of all the possible things that could contribute to an artist's (or anyone's) creativity. Begin with the photos you just looked at. In addition, think of people you know and what they do to increase their creativity. Consider the following categories: setting, food, drink, background noise, time of day, drugs, and so forth.

Freewriting

Think about the creative activities you do. What are they? Where and when do you usually feel the most creative? What in particular inspires you? Write for fifteen minutes without stopping about creativity and you.

Reading for Ideas

The following passage is excerpted from Ernest Hemingway's *A Moveable Feast*, which is Hemingway's account of his life in Paris in the 1920s. In the beginning, he writes about his writing habits. Answer the questions with your classmates and then study the reading.

Prereading Questions

1. Gather information on Ernest Hemingway. When did he live? Where was he born? What was he known for?
2. How do you imagine a writer gets ideas for his or her writing? How do you get your ideas?
3. What do you know about the weather in Paris during the winter?
4. What are mandarins? Chestnuts?

A Moveable Feast

When we came back to Paris it was clear and cold and lovely. . . . Our own apartment was warm and cheerful. . . . The climb to the top floor of the hotel, where I worked in a room that looked across all the roofs and the chimneys of the high hill of the quarter, was a pleasure. The fireplace drew well in the room and it was warm and   5
pleasant to work. I brought mandarins and roasted chestnuts to the room in paper packets, and peeled and ate the small tangerine-like oranges and threw their skins and spat their seeds in the fire when I ate them and roasted chestnuts when I was hungry. I was always

10 hungry with the walking and the cold and the working. Up in the room I had a bottle of kirsch that we had brought back from the mountains and I took a drink of kirsch when I would get toward the end of a story or toward the end of the day's work. When I was through working for the day I put away the notebook, or the paper, in the drawer of
15 the table and put any mandarins that were left in my pocket. They would freeze if they were left in the room at night.

It was wonderful to walk down the long flights of stairs knowing that I'd had good luck working. I always worked until I had something done and I always stopped when I knew what was going to happen
20 next. That way I could be sure of going on the next day. But sometimes when I was starting a new story and I could not get it going, I would sit in front of the fire and squeeze the peel of the little oranges into the edge of the flame and watch the sputter of blue that they made. I would stand and look out over the roofs of Paris and think, "Do
25 not worry. You have always written before and you will write now. All you have to do is write one true sentence. Write the truest sentence that you know." So finally I would write one true sentence, and then go on from there. It was easy then because there was always one true sentence that I knew or had seen or had heard someone say.
30 If I started to write elaborately, or like someone introducing or presenting something, I found that I could cut that scrollwork or ornament out and throw it away and start with the first true simple declarative sentence I had written. Up in that room I decided that I would write one story about each thing that I knew about. I was
35 trying to do this all the time I was writing, and it was good and severe discipline.

It was in that room too that I learned not to think about anything that I was writing from the time I stopped writing until I started again the next day. That way my subconscious would be working on it and
40 at the same time I would be listening to other people and noticing everything, I hoped; learning, I hoped; and I would read so that I would not think about my work and make myself impotent to do it. Going down the stairs when I had worked well, and that needed luck as well as discipline, was a wonderful feeling and I was free then to
45 walk anywhere in Paris.

If I walked down by different streets to the Jardin du Luxembourg in the afternoon I could walk through the gardens and then go to the Musée du Luxembourg where the great paintings were that have now mostly been transferred to the Louvre and the Jeu de Paume.
50 I went there nearly every day for the Cézannes and to see the Manets and the Monets and the other Impressionists that I had first come to know about in the Art Institute of Chicago. I was learning something

from the painting of Cézanne that made writing simple true sentences far from enough to make the stories have the dimensions that I was trying to put in them. I was learning very much from him but I was not articulate enough to explain it to anyone. 55

Ernest Hemingway, *A Moveable Feast* (New York: Bantam Books, 1964), pp. 11–14.

Postreading Questions

Write the answers to questions 1 to 5 on page 137 in the following chart:

Setting: _____

_____

_____

_____

_____

_____

_____

_____

_____

_____

Food/drink: _____

_____

_____

_____

_____

_____

_____

_____

_____

_____

_____

_____

Outside stimuli: _____

_____

_____

_____

_____

_____

_____

1. How did the room where Hemingway worked help him write? How did it contribute to his creativity? How was its location important?

2. Were there particular things that Hemingway ate and drank? What were they?

3. When did Hemingway stop writing each day? Why?

4. When Hemingway ran out of ideas, what did he do for inspiration? Do you think other writers or artists have similar rituals?

5. What objects outside Hemingway's workroom inspired him? How?

Gathering Information

Now conduct some research on one of the artists in the photos or another artist of your choice. Look for information that reveals how the artist gathered ideas for his or her work. What inspired the artist? Organize your research into a chart like the one you did on Hemingway, or in an outline like the one that follows. Give the results of your research to your classmates in a brief presentation. Include the following points.

I. Background about the artist

A. When/where did he or she live?

_____

_____

B. What are/were the artist's special skills/talents?

_____

_____

C. What are the artist's most well-known works?

_____

_____

_____

_____

II. The artist's creative process

A. Does/did the artist work in a special place?

_____

_____

B. Does/did the artist use special tools or materials?

_____

_____

_____

C. Does/did the artist have special rituals?

_____

_____

_____

III. From what/whom does the artist get inspiration?

_____

_____

_____

PART TWO
LANGUAGE FOR WRITING
MAKING COMPARISONS

In the previous section, you learned about the creative process of different artists. When comparing two people or two things, you discuss either their _similarities_ or their _differences_ (and sometimes both). Special expressions are used to describe similarities and differences clearly to the reader. A list of some of the most important expressions for making comparisons follows. Study the different ways of comparing X and Y:

Similarities	Differences
X is as (adjective) as Y.	X is . . . , but Y is. . . .
Both X and Y are. . . .	X is (adjective + *er*) (more [adjective]) than Y.
	X is less (adjective) than Y.
Neither X nor Y is. . . .	X and Y are different.
X can be compared to Y.	X and Y are different in that. . . .
X and Y are alike (in that) they share (certain) characteristics. . . .	X differs from Y in that (because). . . .
X has something in common with Y.	Unlike X, Y is. . . .
X is similar to (like) Y.	Although Even though Whereas While } X is, Y is. . . .

X is similar to Y in that. . . .
Like X, Y is. . . .

Practicing What You've Learned

Exercise 1 Practice these expressions by writing about the artists in the photographs from Part One or the artists you learned about from your classmates' presentations. Write ten sentences using ten different expressions from the preceding list and then exchange your sentences with a partner.

Examples:

My partner and I *are alike in that* we like to write in a coffee shop where we can drink coffee and listen to classical music.

Alice can write for eight hours at a time, *but* Linda can work only for short periods.

1. _____

_____

2. _____

_____

3. _____

_____

4. _____

_____

5. _____

_____

6. _____

_____

7. _____

_____

8. _____

_____

9. _____

_____

10. _____

_____

Exercise 2   Write a paragraph that discusses either the similarities or differences between two artists. Use as many of the comparison expressions as you think are appropriate.

PART THREE

SYSTEMS FOR WRITING

REVIEW OF PARAGRAPH DEVELOPMENT AND ORGANIZATION

In Chapter 3, you saw how to make paragraphs coherent by repeating key words and phrases and by paraphrasing key words and phrases to develop ideas. Another way to establish paragraph coherence is through the use of *sentence connectors,* which link the ideas in one sentence to another. You practiced using sentence connectors in Chapter 3 also. In this chapter, look at sentence connectors that link sentences to each other by indicating similarities or differences. Study the following chart of sentence connectors and their functions.

Sentence Connector	Function	Example
However, In contrast, On the other hand, Conversely,	to indicate differences	Some people require peace and quiet in order to write. *However*, others need the stimulation and excitement of public places.
Similarly, In the same way, Likewise,	to indicate similarities	Poets are often inspired by natural scenery. *Similarly*, artists work in natural settings.

Sentence connectors link independent clauses and usually come between two sentences. However, if the sentences are short, sentence connectors come after a semicolon (;).

Marcel Proust could write only in bed; similarly, it was necessary for Hemingway to do his work in a special place.

Now read the two following paragraphs that compare writing and pottery making. Answer the questions.

a. Both writing and pottery making are crafts that require special skills. The apprentice writer and potter are alike because they learn their skills through instruction and practice. The best instruction comes from studying a master, someone skilled in the craft. The potter must begin by observing the master, then working with the clay himself or herself. The writer begins by reading good writing and by identifying the characteristics that make it good. The potter begins with small projects and then, after gaining skill and confidence, takes on larger projects. The writer starts with short paragraphs before attempting essays. Only after a great deal of practice and careful imitation of master craftsmen can a potter form an object of beauty. Only after writing, rewriting, and studying model works can a writer turn out a successful essay.

b. Writers and potters are similar in that they both learn their crafts by imitating masters, people skilled in the craft. They devote a great deal of time and concentration to following these masters. For example, before the potter can produce a delicate vase or a symmetrical pitcher, he or she must spend time watching a master at work. Likewise, a novice writer cannot produce a well-organized essay or even a coherent paragraph without first studying good models. The potter observes the way the expert spins the wheel and forms the clay; then he or she tries to do exactly what the master has done. Similarly, the apprentice writer imitates the work of a master writer. The potter begins with small, simple projects. In the same way, the writer begins with short paragraphs and proceeds to the essay only after mastering the basics. So just as the potter gains inspiration and skill from an experienced artist, a writer learns to communicate effectively after studying the work of master writers.

1. Which paragraph did you find easier to read? Can you determine why?

   _____

   _____

2. The smoother paragraph (the second one) has sentences that are linked together by sentence connectors. Go back and underline as many sentence connectors as you can find.

Practicing What You've Learned

Practice using the sentence connectors by doing the following exercises.

Exercise 1   Write five sentences about the artists you've learned about in this chapter. Use as many sentence connectors as you can.

   _____

   _____

   _____

   _____

   _____

   _____

   _____

   _____

   _____

   _____

   _____

   _____

   _____

Exercise 2 Using sentence connectors, write five sentences about some of the leisure-time activities discussed in Chapter 6.

_____

_____

_____

_____

_____

_____

_____

_____

_____

_____

_____

ORGANIZING A COMPARISON PARAGRAPH

In Chapters 2 and 4, you studied two different ways of organizing a paragraph. When writing a paragraph that compares or contrasts people or things, the writer usually focuses on either similarities or differences. The topic sentence should state not only that X and Y are similar or different, but, in general, *how* or *why* they are similar or different. In other words, the topic sentence should tell the reader about the basis for comparison. Take a look at the sample topic sentences below:

Incomplete: A writer and a potter *are similar.*

Complete: A writer and a potter *are similar in that* each learns a craft by imitating an expert.

Remember that in academic expository writing, you are trying to convince the reader of an attitude or opinion expressed in the topic sentence. The following points will help you write a stronger paragraph.

1. In a paragraph describing similarities, refer to differences in the topic sentence *only*. In the development, point out only similarities, moving from most important to least important, or least important to most.

2. Similarly, in a paragraph describing differences, discuss similarities only in the topic sentence as a way to lead into the paragraph.

3. There are two ways to organize a comparison paragraph. The first way is to list all the points about X and then all the points about Y. Your paragraph looks like this:

Topic sentence _____

_____
XXXXXXXXXXXXXXXXXXXXXXXXXXXXXXXXXXXXXXXXXX
XXXXXXXXXXXXXXXXXXXXXXXXXXXXXXXXXXXXXXXXXX
On the other hand, YYYYYYYYYYYYYYYYYYYYYYYYYYYYY
YYYYYYYYYYYYYYYYYYYYYYYYYYYYYYYYYYYYYYYYYYY
YYYYYYYYYYYYYYYYYYYYYYYYYYYYYYYYYYYYYYYYYYY

The second way is to describe X and Y for each point of difference or similarity. In this case, the paragraph looks like this:

Topic sentence _____

_____ XXXXXXXXX
YYYYYYYY   XXXXXXX   YYYYYYY   XXXXXX   YYY
YYYY   XXXXXXX   YYYYYYY   XXXXXX   YYYYYY

In addition, you can write a paragraph in which you discuss both the similarities and the differences of X and Y using these same patterns.

Practicing What You've Learned

Exercise 1 Read the following paragraphs. Which pattern of organization does each follow? Which do you prefer? Which seems easier to follow?

a. Writing an essay in Japanese is not as difficult as writing an essay in English because the writing rules are not as strict. Unlike an essay in English, a Japanese essay doesn't have to stick to the topic or have a thesis statement. In English, the ideas should be clearly stated and developed. In Japanese, however, it is acceptable to write vague, subtle, and even ambiguous sentences. In an English essay, the conclusion is in the final part of the paragraph or essay. In contrast, the conclusion in a

Japanese essay can appear at the beginning or the end of the essay, depending on the style. Whereas a Japanese writer can include two or three main ideas in a paragraph, an English writer must limit the paragraph to one. Because the rules are not as strict, it is easier to write an essay in Japanese than in English.[1]

b. Writing letters is more enjoyable than writing compositions. It is fun to write letters to friends and family, as one doesn't have to worry about topic sentences, supporting sentences, or mistakes in grammar. The writer can write about many topics and include as many paragraphs as he or she wants. There is no time limit to writing a letter, so it can be done whenever the writer is in the mood. On the other hand, writing a composition is not as much fun. Each paragraph must begin with a topic sentence and continue with sentences that support it. The writer has to be careful to correct mistakes in grammar and include a paragraph for each supporting idea in the thesis statement. The time for writing a composition is usually restricted, so the writer cannot put it off until he or she feels like doing it. Because of all these rules, writing a composition is much less enjoyable than writing a letter.[2]

Which pattern did Paragraph **a** follow? Paragraph **b?**

Exercise 2   With a partner, choose two artists from Part One and compare or contrast them. Both of you should write about the same things (either similarities or differences) but organize your paragraphs differently. When you've finished, exchange paragraphs and discuss which pattern of organization was the easiest and which was the best suited to the topic.

Assignments

1. Think of two famous artists of any nationality. Choose one aspect of their lives or work and compare it. You might choose to discuss how they are (were) inspired, their workstyles, their writing styles, their subjects, their habits, their lifestyles, or their philosophies. Write a paragraph comparing any aspect of their work.

2. The following quotations, one from a painter and the other from a writer, make similar statements about what takes place during the creative process. Study the quotes to determine what they

---

[1]Rica Kuno
[2]Rafael Garcia

mean, then choose one of them and write a paragraph that compares this approach to creativity to a different approach.

"The picture is not thought out and determined beforehand; rather while it is being made it follows the mobility or thought."
—Picasso

"Think of writing, then, not as a way to transmit a message but as a way to grow and cook a message."—P. Elbow

3. Write a paragraph in which you examine the similarities and/or differences between two of the following creative activities:

writing a song	painting a picture	building a house
writing a poem	sculpting	filmmaking
writing an essay	cooking	designing clothes

PART FOUR

EVALUATING FOR REWRITING

Working with Your Partner

Exchange paragraphs from the assignment in Part Three and answer the following questions.

1. Read the paragraph. Look at it holistically (that is, get a general impression and don't focus on details). What is your impression after one reading?

   a. It's clear—I like it.

   b. I understand what the writer wants to say, but the paragraph isn't smooth.

   c. The paragraph needs to be developed further and the writer needs to include more coherence devices.

2. Look at the details.

   a. Is the topic sentence clear and complete?

   Yes _____   No _____

   If not, what is missing?

   _____

   _____

   _____

   _____

b. Which organizational pattern does the writer use? _____
   Is it effective?

   Yes _____   No _____

c. How many sentence connectors does the writer use? _____

   Should the writer change some of the sentence connectors?

   Yes _____   No _____

   Should the writer add some sentence connectors?

   Yes _____   No _____

   Should the writer omit some sentence connectors?

   Yes _____   No _____

   Specify the changes the writer should make.

   _____

   _____

   _____

d. How many examples of similarities or differences does the
   writer use? _____ What are they?

   _____

   _____

   _____

   Should the writer add more?

   Yes _____   No _____

e. Do you have any further specific comments to help the writer
   improve the paragraph? Write them here:

   _____

   _____

   _____

Working on Your Own

Now you should be ready to evaluate your own paper. Go through
the questions again. Take into consideration what your partner said
about your paper when he or she evaluated it. Is there more to add?
Words to change? Make sure *you* are satisfied before you turn it in
to your teacher.

CHAPTER 8
CHOICES

Antinuclear protest, England.

PART ONE

IDEAS FOR WRITING

CONTROVERSIAL ISSUES

When challenged by a classmate or friend on a controversial issue, can you defend your opinion? Can you provide arguments that help the other person understand your point of view? Do you consider the other person's point of view?

In this chapter, you will examine some controversial issues, state your opinion about them, then defend your opinion in writing. Look at the photos and read each of the accompanying statements. Do you agree or disagree with them? Indicate your opinion by circling the appropriate number on the opinion scale. Discuss your opinions in small groups and give reasons for your answers.

1.

2.

3.

4.

5.

6.

7.

1. Americans are materialistic.

2. More learning takes place in seminars than in large lecture classes.

3. Fathers should take as much responsibility as mothers in raising their children.

4. Americans are obsessed with diet and exercise.

5. It is not necessary for a corporate executive to have technical knowledge of his or her product.

6. Watching t.v. is a waste of time.

7. One cannot learn to be creative; creativity is a natural gift.

Opinion Scale				
Statement	Strongly Agree		→	Strongly Disagree
1.	1	2	3	4
2.	1	2	3	4
3.	1	2	3	4
4.	1	2	3	4
5.	1	2	3	4
6.	1	2	3	4
7.	1	2	3	4

Brainstorming

Study each of the photos in the previous section and think about the themes of the preceding chapters. The statements have more than one side. Think of the other side for each statement and write down the arguments or issues as shown in the following example. Try to come up with as many arguable issues as you can.

Picture/Chapter	Issue
Example:	
1. Culture	Materialism versus spiritual values Possessions versus friends
2. _____	_____
	_____
3. _____	_____
	_____
4. _____	_____
	_____
5. _____	_____
	_____

Picture/Chapter	Issue

6. _____

_____

7. _____

_____

Freewriting

The issues you listed in the chart are provocative and the subject of much debate. Often it is easier to talk and write about something you feel strongly about than an issue on which you are neutral. Choose the one issue you feel strongest about, then discuss your opinion by writing for fifteen minutes without stopping.

Reading for Ideas

Students who major in a liberal arts field are required to develop a background in a variety of subjects: history, pure science, language, and social science. This rule is often called a "breadth requirement," and administrators believe that it is valuable for a student to have background in a broad range of subjects. Students in technical fields, on the other hand, are not always required to fulfill a breadth requirement and they can specialize in their field of study without taking extra courses that do not relate to their major.

Nowadays, many students are choosing to major in technical fields because recent advances in technology are creating more jobs for all types of engineers, computer scientists, and business graduates. The number of liberal arts majors, in contrast, is decreasing. Graduates in history, education, humanities, art, and language are having difficulty finding jobs in their fields.

The following article discusses liberal arts students and claims that they have many advantages that have been overlooked. Before you read the essay, answer the following questions.

Prereading Questions

1. What are liberal arts majors? What are technical majors? Give specific examples of each type.
2. On what basis should a student decide on a major? Should it be on the basis of interest? Job potential? Background offered?

3. If you don't already know, find out which fields your classmates are majoring in. How many of them are in liberal arts fields? Is this a large percentage of the class?

4. What are "communication skills"?

5. In your opinion, is it important for science and technology students to have good communication skills? Why? Why not?

6. What are some advantages to a liberal arts education? What are some disadvantages?

Why a Liberal Arts Major Makes Business Sense

If you're a recent liberal arts graduate who has had to listen to jokes about unemployment from your computer-major classmates, you may have had the last laugh. There are many advantages for the liberal arts major because this high-tech "Information Age" demands people who are flexible and who have good communication skills.   5

There are many liberal arts majors in large corporations who fill important executive positions. For example, a series of research studies conducted by the American Telephone and Telegraph Company of its executives found that liberal arts majors had achieved greater managerial success than those who had technical training   10 or preprofessional majors. Charles L. Brown, chairman of AT&T, said, "We found extremely pertinent evidence that the humanities/social sciences majors are most suited for change, which is the leading feature of the kind of high-speed, high-pressure, high-tech world we now occupy."   15

Liberal arts majors are not only experiencing success in their long-term corporate careers, but they are also finding jobs more easily. A 1982 survey, conducted by the Association of American Colleges, showed that many companies have filled a significant percentage of their entry-level positions with liberal arts graduates.   20 The study showed that the most sought-after quality in a job applicant was communication skills, cited as "very important" by 92 percent of the respondents. Liberal arts majors possess these skills, often without knowing how important they are. It is probably these skills that qualify them for a wide variety of positions, including credit   25 analyst, merchandiser, marketing representative, and human relations manager.

Finally, although some liberal arts majors may still find it more difficult than their technically trained classmates to land that first job, recent graduates report that they don't regret their choice of study.   30

An example is Maryellie Moore, a 1974 graduate who majored in history and is now treasurer of the Matson Navigation Company. She calls history "a very practical major and a terrific background for business." And Margaret Haas, a 1971 East Asian studies graduate who is now a stockbroker, reports, "My studies provided a broad perspective that I need now more and more in my professional life."

Adapted from Grace Hechinger, "Why a Liberal Arts Major Makes Business Sense," *Glamour Magazine* (February 1984).

Postreading Questions

1. According to the writer of this article, what advantages do liberal arts majors have?

_____

_____

_____

2. Why is Maryellie Moore glad that she majored in history? How does Margaret Haas benefit from her major in East Asian studies today?

_____

_____

_____

_____

3. Do you agree with this author? Why or why not?

_____

_____

_____

_____

4. How many different kinds of support does the writer give to defend her point of view? List each type.

_____

_____

_____

_____

5. Is the writer's argument strong? Does she convince you as reader?

_____

6. What counterarguments (arguments against the writer's point of view) could you pose to this author?

_____

_____

_____

_____

_____

_____

Gathering Information

Have you ever seen political debates on television in your country? Have you ever participated in any kind of debate? A debate is a formal discussion of an issue in which two teams or two speakers, each representing a side of an issue, try to convince the audience that their position is the better one. They try to win by speaking clearly about the key points and anticipating counterarguments from the other side. Some college students participate in debates in their academic courses, and others join debate clubs for the enjoyment that oral argument brings and the discipline it requires.

A debate is extremely useful as a prewriting activity because it is similar in format to an argument essay. Study the following chart and compare the parts of a debate to those of an essay. Also, familiarize yourself with the debate terminology.

Debate	Argument Essay
Resolution	Topic
Opening statement	Introduction and thesis statement
First argument and supports; rebuttal	First body paragraph
Second argument and supports; rebuttal	Second body paragraph
Third argument and supports; rebuttal	Third body paragraph
Closing statement	Conclusion

The rebuttal in a debate is where the counterarguments are presented. In an argument essay, the writer does not necessarily have to address the counterarguments for each point.

In addition to having a similar format to an essay, a debate is also formal; therefore, the language used in debating is often similar to written language.

Step 1: As a class, decide on an issue to debate. Select one of the issues you saw in a previous part of this chapter or think of a new one, as long as it is related to the themes presented so far in this text. It must be debatable—that is, it must have two sides and both sides must be plausible. Turn your topic into a resolution and write it on the board. Here is a sample resolution:

Topic: Fathers participating in raising their children.

Resolution: Fathers should take as much responsibility in raising their children as mothers do.

As you can see, this resolution presents the "pro" side of the argument. What is the "con" side?

(Fathers *shouldn't* take as much responsibility. . . .)

Step 2: Now that you have a resolution, divide into pro and con teams. You may wish to join the team that represents your true feelings about the issue, or you may wish to choose the opposite side just for the mental exercise! Every member of each team plays an important role.

Step 3: Read about the duties of the debate team members, then choose one of these roles. If there aren't enough roles for all team members, additional people can help with the note taking, and the argument and rebuttal roles can be taken by two people.

1. *Team captain:* leads the group and presents the opening and closing statements.
2. *Secretary:* takes notes on what everyone says during the planning stage and during the debate itself.
3. *Three people who present arguments:* Each presents one of the main arguments for that side.
4. *Three people who make opposing arguments:* Each presents a counterargument to the three main arguments given by the other side.

Step 4: Gather information to support your side of the topic. Consult resources in the library. Refer to articles, magazines, or books as you would for an essay. Work with your team to develop your opening statement, your main arguments, your rebuttals, and your closing. Take a look at the purpose of each segment of the debate, as outlined under Step 5.

Step 5: The debate itself will take forty-five to sixty minutes. The actual time for each segment can be decided by you and your teacher. Refer to the following format.

Team: Pro and Con

	Purpose	Time
Opening argument	Clearly states team's position on the issue.	1 minute
Three arguments	Represent the three main supports for team's position. Each argument must be developed with facts, statistics, and examples, just like the body of an essay. Facts and statistics are the most important support devices. The argument presenters (as well as the rest of the team) will have to do some research in order to develop convincing arguments.	3 minutes each
Three rebuttals	Counterarguments to the other team's three main arguments. The best way to prepare rebuttals is to try to predict what the other side will use for the three main supports for its position. Then think of the opposing points of view and develop each one as you did for your main arguments. Break time during the debate will allow you to revise the rebuttals if your predictions weren't right.	3 minutes each
Closing statement	Restates your position and winds up the debate.	1 minute

Notice that each part is timed. Three-to-five-minute breaks should be given after each side's arguments so that the persons presenting rebuttals can revise their presentations if necessary.

Step 6: Determine who won the debate by having the presenters and/or the audience vote for the side that was more convincing. This is the time for a follow-up discussion on how you felt the debate went.

PART TWO

LANGUAGE FOR WRITING

EXPRESSING A POINT OF VIEW

Although it is always important for a writer to express a point of view about the essay topic, it is especially important in an argument essay where the topic is usually controversial. You can do this by referring to examples, citing facts, and providing statistics when these types of support are appropriate and when they serve to strengthen your argument.

The following expressions will often be useful when you state an opinion. Study them and note how they are used in a sentence.

have to + verb	Liberal arts majors *have to study* a broad range of subjects to meet graduation requirements.
	A liberal arts major *has to study* a broad range of subjects.
need to + verb	Students *need to think* about the job market when choosing a major.
	A student *needs to think* about the job market when choosing a major.

(Notice that the verbs in these expressions must agree with the subjects; that is, they must be conjugated.)

should + verb	Advisors *should not discourage* students from majoring in liberal arts fields.
must + verb	College graduates, no matter what major, *must have* communication skills to secure a good job.
ought to + verb	If a student decides to major in business or engineering, he or she *ought to be* sure he or she has good communication skills.

Practicing What You've Learned

1. Write five of your own sentences using these expressions. Choose the issue you wrote about in "Freewriting" as your topic.
2. Now, combine the sentences into a coherent and unified paragraph.

EXPOSING THE OTHER SIDE: PREDICTING THE OUTCOME

In an argument essay, it is often effective to disprove or discredit the other side of the argument in conditional sentences. You can do this by using sentences with result clauses. Read the following examples:

1. Engineering graduates lose precious job opportunities if they don't have good communication skills.

2. If science students do not learn effective writing techniques, it will be difficult for them to express their ideas correctly.

3. If a student chooses a liberal arts major instead of a technical major, he or she will probably learn good communication skills.

Note that each of these sentences can be divided into two parts. One part is called the *condition clause* (introduced by *if*) and the other part is called the *result clause*. Answer the following questions about Sentences 1 through 3.

1. Note the position of the *if* condition clause. Does it come at the beginning of the sentence or at the end?

   _____

2. Note the punctuation of the sentences. Can you hypothesize something about the position of the *if* condition clause and the use of commas?

   _____

   _____

3. Reread the *if* condition clauses in the sentences again. In terms of their *function* in an argument, what do they all have in common?

   _____

   _____

4. Note the verb tense used in the *if* condition clauses. Is it always the same? What tense is it?

   _____

If your answers to these questions were correct, you noted that condition clauses can come at either the beginning or the end of a sentence, but if they appear at the beginning, they are separated from the result clause by a comma. If they appear at the end, no punctuation is necessary. You also noted that the three condition clauses in Sentences 1 through 3 refer to the opposing point of view exclusively. In addition, they're all in the present tense.

Another way to write Sentences 1 through 3 is to use relative clauses. Read the following examples.

1. Engineering graduates who lack good communication skills lose precious job opportunities.

2. Science students who are poor in writing can't express their ideas correctly.

3. A student who chooses a liberal arts major will learn good communication skills.

Practicing What You've Learned

Exercise 1   Complete the following sentences by providing the missing clause or by rewriting the sentence with a relative clause. Your point of view for this exercise is that of the writer in Part One ("Why a Liberal Arts Major Makes Business Sense"). Don't forget to add punctuation when necessary.

Example: if scientists lack skill in reading . . .

If scientists lack skill in reading, they won't be able to keep up with their colleagues.

Scientists who lack skill in reading will not be able to keep up with their colleagues.

1. if an accomplished engineer cannot write effectively _____

_____

_____

2. if science and technology students don't study English _____

_____

_____

3. it will be harder for him to get a promotion _____

_____

_____

4. she will be less effective at her job _____

_____

_____

5. a job applicant's inability to express himself is immediately apparent _____

_____

_____

Exercise 2   Now write five sentences of your own, but take the *opposite* point of view. In other words, argue against a liberal arts major. Try to vary the sentences as much as possible. Exchange sentences with a partner and check each other's work when you finish.

Example: If students majoring in science and technology take English courses, they won't be able to concentrate on their major course.

_____

_____

_____

_____

_____

_____

_____

_____

_____

Exercise 3   Finally, write five sentences about the issue you selected from Part One in "Freewriting." Remember to include the opposing point of view in condition clauses.

_____

_____

_____

_____

_____

_____

_____

_____

_____

_____

_____

_____

PART THREE

SYSTEMS FOR WRITING

FROM PARAGRAPH TO ESSAY: THE EXPOSITORY ESSAY

In this part, you're going to take a look at how ideas you've previously expressed in paragraphs can be expanded and developed into entire essays. You're also going to look at the components of the short essay and how they function to communicate your ideas fully in an academic setting.

Review the essay about liberal arts in Part One. What arguments *against* majoring in the liberal arts could you and your classmates think of? Perhaps one of your arguments against a liberal arts major is that the broad background demanded by "breadth requirements" makes it difficult for students to specialize in a particular field. The writer of the following paragraph believes this. As you will see, she thinks students interested in science and technical fields should be able to concentrate on science and technical courses *only* and should not be required to take courses in other fields. Read the paragraph and answer the questions. Notice how the writer defends her point of view.

Science students should not be required to take English courses because they won't necessarily use these English skills in their field. English courses require a great deal of time, and these courses will force science students to shift their focus away from the more important science courses. Because scientists are required to write reports and are concerned with numerical data, English literature or composition courses are not useful to them. Furthermore, science students have limited time in which to complete both general and specialized courses for their majors, and unnecessary English courses consume precious time that is better spent on a course related to their fields. Family, science courses focus on systematic and practical knowledge, whereas English courses emphasize imagination and creative expression. The differences in focus and purpose between science and English courses distract the busy science student. These three reasons clearly show that science students should not have to take English courses.[1]

---

[1] Yunsun Cho

163

1. What is the main idea of the paragraph?

_____

_____

_____

2. What reasons does the writer give to support her main idea?

_____

_____

_____

_____

_____

3. Do you think the information in this paragraph could be expanded into a longer paragraph or even an essay? Why? Why not?

_____

_____

_____

So far, you have been explaining and illustrating your ideas in paragraphs. Now you are going to learn to expand a paragraph into an essay. As a college student, you often will be required to write essays. In academic expository essays, like paragraphs, the writer states an attitude or opinion about an issue and then supports and defends his or her opinion. Sometimes the writer is explaining or describing something, stating one side of an argument and proving it, or showing the relationship between two things. An academic expository essay is at least four paragraphs long, with the main discussion (called _body_ or _middle_ paragraphs) preceded by an introduction and followed by a conclusion. The writer generally includes a statement of his or her main idea for the entire essay (called the _thesis statement_) at the end of the introductory paragraph. The thesis statement (which will be discussed in more depth in Chapter 9) is important because it prepares the reader from the beginning for everything that is to follow in the essay.

Because almost any paragraph can be viewed as a mini-essay, the progression from paragraph to essay is a logical one. A well-written paragraph contains ideas that can be further developed into additional paragraphs if the writer does a little more thinking and research on the topic.

Now go back and review the paragraph that discusses why science students shouldn't take English courses. Then read the following

five-paragraph essay on the same topic and answer the questions.
As you read the essay, notice how the ideas in the paragraph have
been expanded. Also notice the way in which the ideas have been
organized.

Science Students and English Requirements

People who want to be at the top in their field have much more
competition today than ever before; therefore, they must work harder
to get to the top. To truly excel, they must devote as much time as
possible to gaining sufficient theoretical background and practical
experience in their fields. They must not be distracted by subjects
and activities that have little or no relation to their chosen fields.
Therefore, it is important that science students not be required to take
intensive English courses. The uselessness of English in their fields,
the lack of time for such study, and the difference in focus of an
English course are reasons why science students should be freed
from studying English.

Students majoring in science should not be required to study
English because they won't have to use it in their majors. Scientists
in general do not have to write or speak much during the course
of their academic studies because most of their studies are based
on scientific observation, measurement, and research. Their papers
are factual or numerical and do not have to be imaginative. Therefore,
English composition or literature courses are not useful in scientific
fields of study. In addition, information that is not immediately
applicable will be quickly forgotten. So because science students
cannot apply English immediately, they likely won't be able to retain
what they have learned for long-range application. Therefore,
because their fields of study do not require precision in English skills,
science students should not have to take English courses.

A second reason why science students shouldn't be required to
take English classes is the limited time they have in school. They
usually have so many requirements to fulfill that they are usually much
busier than students majoring in the liberal arts. Furthermore, these
requirements are often courses that are not related to their science
majors. For example, science majors at my university must take a
history course and fulfill a foreign language requirement in addition
to taking English. These nonrelated courses distract the students
so that they cannot concentrate on their majors. They prevent science
students from pursuing research in their fields. They force them to
waste precious time on courses they will not use.

Finally, science focuses on very systematic and practical knowledge, whereas English emphasizes original ideas and creative expression. Science is objective, whereas writing is subjective. The two subjects have opposite emphases and serve to confuse the student.

In summary, science students should not be required to take English courses because they will not use the skills they learn in English courses, they have no time for courses unrelated to their fields, and the focus of English courses distracts and confuses them. Future scientists need to spend their time concentrating on their majors in order to contribute to society. Only without the unnecessary extra courses will they be able to benefit society in the long run and gain professional satisfaction from their work.

Yun Sun Cho

1. What parts of the essay are the same as or similar to the paragraph?

_____

_____

_____

2. What parts of the essay are new?

_____

_____

_____

3. Where were these new parts added?

_____

_____

_____

4. Why were the new parts added?

_____

_____

_____

Look at the diagram, which shows how the parts of the paragraph relate to those of an essay:

Paragraph   Essay

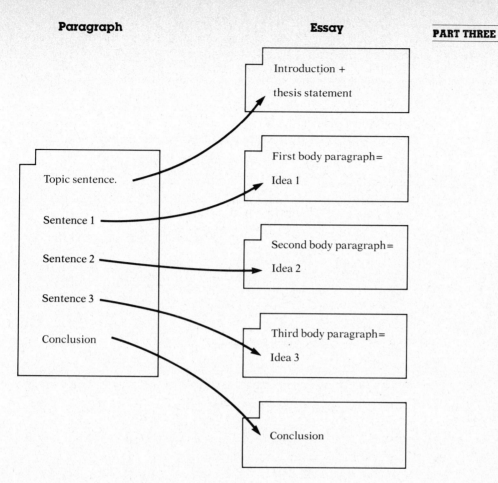

Practicing What You've Learned

Exercise 1 Complete the following outline based on the essay you just read.

I. Introduction and thesis statement

_____

_____

_____

II. First idea

_____

_____

_____

III. Second idea

_____

_____

_____

IV. Third idea

_____

_____

_____

V. Conclusion

_____

_____

_____

Exercise 2 Expand this paragraph into an essay by completing the three steps that follow.

   Students majoring in science and technical fields must learn communication skills because both during their academic careers and after graduation, they need to know how to read efficiently, write well, and communicate effectively. Both students and employees have large amounts of material to read. They must be able to read this material quickly and distinguish the important points from the less important points. In addition, clear writing is essential both before and after graduation. Ideas and experiments need to be recorded, and without good writing skills students lose grade points and workers lose credibility on the job. Finally, effective communication through speaking is essential for students to understand lectures and for employees to secure jobs and advances.

Step 1: Make an outline in note form of the paragraph.

Write the topic sentence here: _____

_____

_____

What is Idea 1? _____

_____

_____

What is Idea 2? _____

_____

_____

_____

What is Idea 3? _____

_____

_____

_____

Step 2: Based on your experience and the reading you've done in this chapter and in previous chapters, add supporting information to each of the ideas. Use examples, facts, statistics, or anecdotes. Jot down your supporting points in the space provided under each idea in Step 1.

Step 3: Now write an essay based on your outline. Remember that the paragraphs, although part of an essay, should contain all the elements you've been practicing in the book up to this point.

Exercise 3 Expand one of the paragraphs you wrote in a previous chapter into a four- or five-paragraph essay. First, make an outline like the one in Exercise 2.

Assignments

Each of these assignments requires writing a four- or five-paragraph essay.

1. Write an essay in which you argue for or against the issue you debated in class.

2. Choose an issue in Part One that interests you and argue for one side or the other. You may also choose one of the topics you brainstormed for.

   Americans are materialistic.

   More learning takes place in seminars than in large lecture classes.

   Fathers should take as much responsibility as mothers in raising their children.

   Americans are obsessed with diet and exercise.

   It is not necessary for corporate executives to have technical knowledge of their product.

   Watching t.v. is a waste of time.

   One cannot learn to be creative.

3. Write an essay in which you argue for or against a liberal arts major. Make sure that you use different reasons to support your point of view than those already presented in this chapter.

4. Agree with, disagree with, or explain one of the following quotations:

"Education is one of the chief obstacles to intelligence and freedom of thought."—Bertrand Russell

"If you reject the food, ignore the customs, fear the religion, and avoid the people, you might better stay home. You are like a pebble thrown into water; you become wet on the surface but you are never a part of the water."—James Michener

PART FOUR

EVALUATING FOR REWRITING

In this section, you are going to evaluate your classmate's and your own first attempt at writing a short essay. Most of the things that you are going to evaluate (essay form, thesis statement) will be discussed in much more detail in later chapters. Don't worry if you don't completely understand all of the elements of an essay. At this point, you just need to have a feeling for the overall structure of the essay and how the supporting ideas in an essay are similar to those in a paragraph.

Working with Your Partner

Exercise 1   How many paragraphs does the essay have? _____

Exercise 2   Locate each part of the essay and indicate which paragraph it corresponds to:

Introduction   Paragraph number _____

Body   Paragraph number _____

                    Paragraph number _____

                    Paragraph number _____

Conclusion   Paragraph number _____

Are there any parts in the essay that do not correspond to one of the essay parts above?

Yes _____   No _____

If the answer is *yes*, consider whether this part should be eliminated or incorporated into another part of the essay.

Exercise 3 Is there a thesis statement (a sentence that tells you what the entire essay is to be about)? If so, underline it. Does it *really* prepare you for the essay that follows?

Yes _____   No _____

If the answer is *no*, how could you improve the thesis statement?

Exercise 4 Put an *X* next to the topic sentences of each body paragraph. Does each topic sentence meet the criteria discussed in Chapter 1?

Yes _____   No _____

If the answer is *no* for any of the topic sentences, how could you improve it?

Exercise 5 Are the ideas in each of the body paragraphs developed fully according to what you already know about good paragraph development?

Yes _____   No _____

If the answer is *no* for any of the body paragraphs, how could you develop it more fully?

Working on Your Own

Now you should be ready to evaluate your own essay. Go through the questions again, keeping in mind what your partner said about your essay when he or she evaluated it. Pay particular attention to the form. Does it have all the necessary parts? Is there a statement that tells the reader what the essay is about? If you feel that you understand the general idea of what a short essay is, congratulations!

CHAPTER 9
THE PHYSICAL WORLD

Arctic landscape.

1.

2.

3.

4.

5.

6.

PART ONE

IDEAS FOR WRITING

ENVIRONMENT AND CULTURE

The great variety in geographical features around the world is astounding: the high mountains of Tibet, the ice and snow of the arctic regions, the lush jungles of South America, the flat open spaces of the Middle West of the United States. Have you ever wondered what life is like for the people who live in a region that is very different from yours? What effect does geography have on the culture and history of a group of people? Do geographical differences cause cultural differences? You're going to consider these ideas in this chapter. Begin by studying these photos of various parts of the world and their inhabitants and then answering the questions.

1. What parts of the world do these photos represent? If you're not sure, guess.

_____

_____

_____

_____

_____

_____

_____

2. How do these areas of the world differ from each other?

_____

_____

_____

_____

_____

_____

3. What are the unique environmental features (natural or man-made) of each one?

_____

_____

_____

_____

_____

_____

_____

_____

_____

_____

Brainstorming

In small groups, make notes about all of the facts you are aware of about the people who live in these parts of the world. Think about what kind of work they do, what they eat, what they wear, what kind of art they are noted for, their religion, their political and social systems, and anything else you can think of. Use the following chart.

Photo	Location	Work	Food	Clothing	Social System	Other
1.						
2.						
3.						
4.						
5.						

Photo	Location	Work	Food	Clothing	Social System	Other
6. _____	_____	_____	_____	_____	_____	_____
_____	_____	_____	_____	_____	_____	_____

Freewriting

Write for fifteen minutes without stopping about the physical environment of the area that you come from. Is it urban or rural? What geographical features are there? Mountains? Desert? Lakes? Is it near the ocean? What is the weather like? What manmade features is it known for? Tall buildings? Ancient ruins?

   Alternate assignment: Describe your region briefly and try to examine how the region itself has influenced your culture. Again, write for fifteen minutes without stopping.

Reading for Ideas

The following is an excerpt from *Never in Anger: Portrait of an Eskimo Family*. The author, Jean L. Briggs, is a Canadian anthropologist who wanted to learn about Eskimo culture. To do this, she made friends with an Eskimo family in the Utku tribe who agreed to let her live with them as one of the family. In a sense, she was "adopted" by them. She became very close to her Eskimo family and even refers to the members as "my father," "my sister," and so forth. In this selection, she describes how the Utku feel about having to move frequently because of their harsh environment. As you read the passage, try to guess meanings of new words from context; notice the poetic language the author sometimes uses to describe the Eskimos' land.

Prereading Questions

1. In what part of the world do Eskimos live?
2. Describe the region in which they live in as much detail as you can.
3. What do Eskimos eat?
4. What do they wear?
5. What is a *nomad?*
6. What is an *igloo?*

Never in Anger: Portrait of an Eskimo Family

Nomadic life is very pleasurable for the Utku. Difficult as moving sometimes is—when the sled runners run into snowdrifts and stick, when the river-snow becomes soaked with water so that dogs and people slosh deep in slush and are soon drenched, when winds bite at noses and toes so that the children tied atop the load cry with cold or shrink silently into the protective quilts wrapped around them—nevertheless, a move to a new campsite is a memorable break in the ordinary flow of life. People look forward to the change of scene or of dwelling, just as they look forward to each changing season. In the autumn, the talk is about how good it will feel to move into an igloo. The night before we set off for Amujat,[1] my first October at Back River, Inuttiaq, my Eskimo father, lying in bed, gestured in the air the motions of cutting snow blocks and sang a little song about tomorrow's igloo building. In the spring, when the igloos have been transformed by long occupancy into small caves of dirty grey ice, the talk turns to the pleasures of the spring moves: "Igloos are unpleasant in the spring," they say. "The water of Amujat tastes unpleasantly of salt; it will be good to go to Itimnaaqjuk[1] and fish." And people pantomime the motions of fishing for trout through the ice.

Even the process of moving holds excitement. A happy bustle of activity pervades a camp that is preparing to move. Packing is done at a double-quick tempo, orders given and obeyed with an energy rarely seen in the quiet life of a settled camp. In the spring, when thawing weather and the search for fish required frequent moves, the spirit of impermanence seemed to infect people, so that, from my point of view, they seemed to make the maximum rather than the minimum necessary number of moves. At this season, unlike any other, tents were shifted for the slightest reason: because the gravel floor had become soiled with bits of paper and fishbones, or because a change in the wind was filling the tent with mosquitoes. Shifting was not done for such small reasons in the more permanent summer camp; there, the unwanted foreign matter was picked out of the gravel and the mosquitoes were simply endured. In spring, too, when the flooding river forced us uphill, the retreat was always made foot by foot as the river rose. For several days we moved camp at least once a day and sometimes more often, and always when the water had arrived within inches of our doorsteps. Once as we were setting up the tents for the third or fourth time, I asked the friend who was helping me: "Does the water come up this high?" (I indicated the spot

[1]Names of places in the region

where we were placing the tents.) "Sometimes it does and sometimes it doesn't," was the answer.

I do not know what made people move this way. It may have been optimism; weakened by measles, as the Utku were that spring, they may have hoped that each small move would be the last. But then why shift the tent to escape the mosquitoes or improve the flooring? It sometimes seemed as though rearranging the environment by moving were a form of play for the Eskimos, a pleasure in itself. Whatever the explanation, I never completely shared the Eskimo spirit. I found it a trying job to pull up a tent, move all its contents uphill in my arms, set up the tent again and rearrange the interior. Once it was done, I enjoyed the freshness of a new home, a tent floor carpeted with reindeer moss and cranberry blossoms[2]. Still, moves were a nuisance that upset my work and, worse, made me feel disoriented in my environment. So, in moving away from the rising water, if I could have done what I wanted, I would have moved, once and for all, the few hundred feet to the top of the hill and sat there securely, looking down at the flood.

The fact that the moves were always made with no time to spare I sometimes found a little disturbing, too. I was never quite sure when I went to bed with the water two feet from my door whether I was going to wake up floating. One such evening I remarked to Inuttiaq that the dogs, who were chained to boulders at the water's edge, were going to get wet during the night. "Yes, they are," he said. And sure enough, in the morning several dogs were standing belly-deep in the flood, their noses pointing stiffly skyward.

In the course of many years of moving up and down the river, from campsite to campsite, from one fishing place to another, the countryside that seemed so limitless to me and at first sight so empty, had become to its inhabitants as marked with familiar associations as a friend's face. It may be partly the recognition of these landmarks together with the excitement of change that gives the Utku pleasure in their way of life. Like other wandering people, the Utku have a remarkable memory for the details of their territory, and the accuracy with which they observe and mentally record the shape of the terrain and their skill in making and reading maps are phenomenal. I showed several Utku men maps of the entire North American Arctic. They pointed out and named correctly all the major rivers, lakes, and islands in a territory approximately 135,000 miles square.

Adapted from Jean L. Briggs, *Never in Anger: Portrait of an Eskimo Family* (Cambridge: Harvard University Press), 1970, pp. 32–34.

---

[2]Plants found in this region

Postreading Questions

1. Describe the Utkus' attitude toward their nomadic lifestyle.

   _____

   _____

   _____

   _____

   _____

2. Does the author know *why* the Utkus feel the way they do about moving?

   _____

3. Why do the Utkus move from their igloos in the spring?

   _____

   _____

   _____

4. Why else do the Utkus move from place to place?

   _____

   _____

   _____

5. Describe the Utkus' relationship with their territory.

   _____

   _____

   _____

   _____

6. What didn't the author like about moving? Why do you think she felt this way?

   _____

   _____

   _____

   _____

7. Would you enjoy a nomadic lifestyle? Why? Why not?

_____

_____

_____

_____

_____

8. Name some other nomadic groups in the world.

_____

_____

_____

_____

Gathering Information

A *scavenger hunt* is a game in which the players, in teams, must find unusual objects or answers to difficult questions. The team that finishes first and has the most correct items wins. The following is a scavenger hunt in which you find answers to difficult questions about how environment affects the cultures of the world. The purpose is to get more information about the topic of environment and culture in an exciting way.

Divide into teams or pairs. Try to be the first group to have all correct answers to the following questions. You may interview classmates, friends, professors at your school, or others, and you may do library research. You will notice that some of the following questions are more difficult than others, and some of them are actually groups of questions on the same topic. Answer the questions by working with other students on your team.

1. Name an ethnic group noted for longevity. How is this longevity influenced by the environment in which these people live?

_____

_____

_____

2. How many words are there for *snow* in the Eskimo language?

_____

_____

3. What does *fulfillment of our manifest destiny* mean? What, if anything, does it have to do with American culture?

_____

_____

_____

4. How many uses did the American Plains Indians have for the buffalo? What were they?

_____

_____

_____

5. Which five cities have the greatest population density? How did these cities become so large? What can you say about the people who live in these cities? How has the size of each city affected the lives and attitudes of its inhabitants?

_____

_____

_____

_____

_____

6. Which five countries in the world have the largest populations? For each country, find out whether its inhabitants all speak the same language and explain how this phenomenon affects the people's lives and cultures.

_____

_____

_____

_____

_____

7. Find one religion in which a natural phenomenon (a mountain, the sea, and so forth) plays an important part. Explain the significance of this phenomenon in the religion.

_____

_____

_____

_____

8. What are the five longest rivers in the world? Choose three and explain how life in these areas is affected by the river.

_____

_____

_____

9. Describe the attitudes and lifestyles of people who live on the Hawaiian Islands. Consider both the native Polynesians and the Americans and Europeans who have settled there. How does their geographical setting influence their behavior?

_____

_____

_____

10. Which area of the world has the greatest rainfall? The least? How do these conditions affect the people who live in these areas?

_____

_____

_____

PART TWO

LANGUAGE FOR WRITING

DESCRIBING ENVIRONMENTAL CONDITIONS

In your assignments for this chapter, you are going to consider the effects of environmental conditions on human culture. Therefore, words and expressions that describe environmental conditions, climate, and geography will be useful to you. How many of these words and expressions do you already know?

Look at each of the environmental terms in the boxes that follow and write all the words and expressions that come into your mind as you see each word. Write down anything that you think of, but make sure that what you write is related to the original word. Notice that you can use nouns, verbs, adjectives, or other expressions.

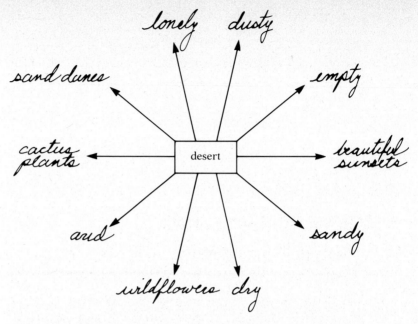

Now use these words to draw vocabulary diagrams like the preceding one:

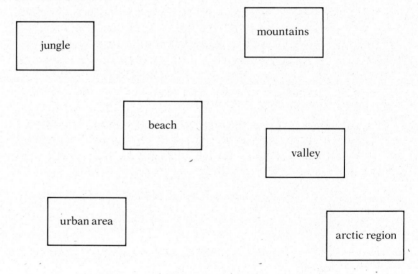

Practicing What You've Learned

1. Choose one group of words that you just wrote down, and use them in a paragraph about that region (mountains, arctic region, valley, or whatever).

2. Write another paragraph in which you discuss one of the regions of the world shown in the photographs in Part One. Use the vocabulary from this section and consider the inhabitants of the region and how their environment influences their attitudes and lifestyles.

PART THREE

SYSTEMS FOR WRITING

THE THESIS STATEMENT → main idea

↓idea

The sentence that expresses the main idea of an essay is called the *thesis statement*. A thesis statement, by expressing the main idea, prepares the reader for what is to follow. In this way, it performs the same function as the topic sentence (see Chapter 1) but covers an entire essay rather than a single paragraph. Like the topic sentence, it contains a statement of the writer's *approach* to the topic he or she is writing about. That is, a thesis statement announces the topic and presents the ideas that will *support* or *prove* this point of view. A thesis that only announces the topic is not complete; the supporting ideas *must* be included also. All of this is done in one complete sentence that appears at the end of the first paragraph in the essay. The following is a thesis statement taken from a four-paragraph essay about the attitudes and lifestyles of Europeans who live in the Hawaiian Islands. Study the thesis statement and answer the questions.

The climate of the Hawaiian Islands affects the Europeans who have settled there in the way they dress and in the way they perceive time.

1. Find the part of the thesis statement that expresses the topic of the essay and underline it. about climate

2. Find the ideas in the thesis that support the topic. How many are there? Write them here.

_____

_____

_____

_____

185

3. Suppose for a moment that this thesis sentence is the answer to a question. From the following list, choose the question that the thesis statement is an answer to:

_____ Are the Europeans who have settled in the Hawaiian Islands affected by the climate there?

___✕___ How are the Europeans who have settled in the Hawaiian Islands affected by the climate there?

_____ How does European dress change with life in the Hawaiian Islands?

4. Based on your understanding of this thesis statement, what do you think the essay it comes from is about?

_____

_____

_____

_____

Like a topic sentence, a thesis sentence is usually an answer to one or more information questions (*who, what, why, in what way, how,* and so forth). It can be outlined in the following way:

Announcement of Topic:

The climate of the Hawaiian Islands affects Europeans who have settled there.

Supporting Idea 1: in the way they dress

Supporting Idea 2: in the way they perceive time

Explain why the following is not a thesis statement:

Island life affects the attitudes of Hawaiians in two main ways.

As you probably noticed, this thesis statement is missing an important part: the supporting ideas.
    To summarize, a good thesis statement:

- gives the reader a clear idea of what the essay will be about.
- has two main parts: the point of view (or announcement of the topic) and the supporting ideas or reasons for the point of view.
- has supporting ideas that answer one or more information questions: *who, what, in what way, how, why, when, where,* and so forth.

Here are some more points to remember about the thesis statement:

1. Your point of view (or announcement of the topic) is not necessarily stated as a personal opinion in your thesis statement,

although it can be. For example, in some cases your thesis can begin with:

"In my opinion, Hawaiians. . . ."

You usually can express a personal opinion when the topic or the writing assignment specifically calls for it.

2. Mention in your thesis only what you can realistically cover in your essay. Choose a point of view that can be discussed in a four-to-five-paragraph essay and supporting ideas that can be adequately developed in one paragraph.

3. Each supporting idea for your thesis should be limited enough to be developed in one paragraph and should have the same degree of generality. In other words, don't use a rather general support with a very specific one. These supporting ideas have the same degree of generality:

"The influences of a desert environment are expressed in Navajo culture through the *clothing* they wear and the *food* they eat."

These don't:

"The Hunzas' longevity is due to *heredity* and the fact that *they don't smoke*." ↓ long life   *healthy style of life*

As you can see, this thesis is out of balance because *heredity* is a wide topic and *not smoking* is a comparatively specific one.

Practicing What You've Learned

Exercise 1 Read the following thesis statements and decide which are good and which aren't, according to the preceding guidelines about thesis statements. For each inadequate thesis statement, be prepared to explain *why* it is inadequate and to rewrite it to make it better. Work with one or two partners.

1. Higher education is a waste of time. ✓ more specific. ✗

2. There are three main differences between U.S. culture and Japanese culture. ✓

3. Research has shown that people will live longer if they avoid stress and don't eat sugar. ✗

4. Smaller university classes are more conducive to learning than large ones because students get more individual attention and they have more opportunities to participate in class. ✓

5. There are many examples of the influences of environment on cultural values in myths and religion. ✗

Exercise 2 Many times in academic courses, students are asked to write a paper that explores a question posed by the professor. In addition, students must often take essay exams to demonstrate how much they've learned. An essay exam is one in which the student writes a short essay in response to a question, usually in a limited amount of time. Therefore, it's a good idea to learn how to quickly form a focused point of view with specific supporting ideas. To practice this, read the following questions and write a thesis statement in response to each one. You may wish to set a time limit in which to do this exercise.

1. Should science and technology students be required to take communication skills courses in college?

   _____

   _____

   _____

2. What are the major differences between your culture and American culture?

   _____

   _____

   _____

   _____

3. Should fathers assume as much responsibility in raising their children as mothers do?

   _____

   _____

   _____

4. What is success?

   _____

   _____

   _____

5. What are the main causes of poor health among college students?

   _____

   _____

   _____

6. What is intelligence?

_____

_____

7. Do the positive effects of advanced technology outweigh the negative effects?

_____

_____

_____

8. How does environment affect culture?

_____

_____

_____

9. Why do people who live in warm climates tend to be more relaxed?

_____

_____

_____

10. What are some of the effects of living in a crowded urban area?

_____

_____

_____

When you finish, exchange your thesis statements with a partner and check each other's work according to the guidelines already presented. Make suggestions for improvement.

Exercise 3 In this exercise, you are going to practice developing thesis statements.

Step 1: Form small groups or work with the entire class. Choose a secretary to take notes on what is said during the brainstorming session. Your teacher will assign one of the essays in the following "Assignments" section. Read it carefully to make sure you understand it.

Step 2: Now, call out everything and anything that comes into your mind that you associate with this topic. (The "secretary" will write all this down.) Don't be shy and don't hold anything back because you think it's silly or off the topic. Do this for about fifteen to twenty minutes.

Step 3: Examine the ideas in your list. Do you detect a pattern? Is there one main idea that seems more significant than any other? Pick out the most important idea in the list. Could this be your point of view on the essay topic? Can you discuss it adequately in four to five paragraphs? If so, underline it twice.

Step 4: Now, look in your list for two to three other ideas that are related to your point of view and, at the same time, can be developed to support or prove it. Are these ideas of the same level of generality? Can they each be discussed in one paragraph? Do they answer an information question about the point of view? If you answered *yes* to these questions, circle these supporting ideas.

Step 5: Combine your point of view and your supporting ideas into one complete, clear statement. Now you have a thesis statement.

Step 6: Evaluate your thesis according to the guidelines presented at the beginning of Part Three. (If you've been working in groups, give your thesis to another group.) If it passes, you're ready to move on.

Don't throw your notes away! They're a valuable source of details, examples, and illustrations for use in developing your supporting ideas. Pick out specific details that are related to each of your supporting ideas. Make sure the details are relevant, concrete, and clear. See how easy it is to get started on a writing assignment? You may even have found that the brainstorming process helped develop your point of view on the topic.

Assignments

1. Discuss the effects of the environmental features of a particular part of the world on the people who live there. Use the information you gathered in Part One.

2. Compare two different regions of the world. In your comparison, consider the environmental features and how they affect the inhabitants.

3. Write an essay in which you answer one of the following questions:

   Why do people who live in warm climates tend to be more relaxed?

   What are some of the effects of living in a crowded urban area?

What effect does environment have on the longevity of a group of people?

4. Agree with, disagree with, or explain the following quotation:

"There is no solitude in the world like that of the big city."
—Kathleen Norris

PART FOUR
EVALUATING FOR REWRITING
Working with Your Partner

Evaluate your partner's essay by answering the following questions.

1. Read only the first paragraph of the essay. Locate the thesis statement and write it in the following space:

Thesis statement: _____

_____

_____

2. Does it have a point of view? Underline it twice. Are there supporting ideas? Circle them.

3. Is the point of view limited enough to be discussed in a four-to-five-paragraph essay?

Yes _____   No _____

If the answer is *no*, make suggestions for revision.

_____

_____

_____

4. Look at the supporting ideas again. Write them here, then answer the following questions.

Supporting idea 1: _____

_____

Supporting idea 2: _____

_____

Supporting idea 3: _____

_____

a. Do each of the supporting ideas answer an information question about the point of view? What are the information questions?

1. _____

_____

2. _____

_____

3. _____

_____

b. Is each of the supporting ideas limited enough to be developed in one paragraph of the essay?

Yes _____   No _____

If the answer is *no*, make suggestions for revision.

c. Do all of the supporting ideas have the same degree of generality?

Yes _____   No _____

If the answer is *no*, make suggestions for revision.

5. Now, describe in a couple of sentences what you think the essay is about, based on the thesis sentence. (Don't read the rest of the essay yet!)

_____

_____

_____

_____

6. Now read the rest of the essay. Was your description in Question 5 correct?

Yes _____   No _____

If the answer is *no*, explain why the thesis statement did not prepare you for the essay and make suggestions for revision.

_____

_____

_____

7. Rate the entire essay, keeping in mind all the material you've learned in this chapter, as well as in previous chapters.

Rating	The essay . . .
1	needs major revisions.
2	is good in parts, but the thesis statement and/or the overall organization is unclear.
3	is very good; the thesis is clear, the organization is easy to follow, and the ideas are well developed.

Working on Your Own

Now you should be ready to evaluate your own essay. Go through the questions again. Take into consideration what your partner said about your thesis statement when he or she evaluated it. Does it adequately prepare the reader for what is to follow? Is it clear? Is anything missing? Finally, score your own essay before you turn it in to the teacher. Did you earn a 3?

CHAPTER 10
HUMAN BEHAVIOR

1.

2.

3.

4.

5.

6.

PART ONE

IDEAS FOR WRITING

NONVERBAL BEHAVIOR

Have you ever noticed that some people communicate with their hands and other parts of the body more or less than others? How much information do you think people can communicate without language? The following pictures show people communicating without words. Describe what the people in the pictures are doing. What does their behavior mean? What country do you think they are from?

Brainstorming

Analyze these photos further by making some comparisons. Would you find the behavior in the photos in your culture? If so, what would it mean? How could it lead to cross-cultural misunderstanding? Discuss these questions in small groups and record your answers in the following chart.

Photo	What are they doing?	Where are they from?	What can this mean in another country?	Misunderstanding?
1. ___				
2. ___				
3. ___				
4. ___				
5. ___				
6. ___				

197

Freewriting

Can you think of an example of nonverbal behavior in your country that is interpreted differently in the United States or Canada? Consider facial expressions, gestures, or how people perceive time and space. Write for fifteen minutes without stopping and describe your example in as much detail as possible.

Reading for Ideas

The following is an excerpt from an article entitled "Nonverbal Behavior: Some Intricate and Diverse Dimensions in Intercultural Communication" by Fathi S. Yousef. Professor Yousef is a specialist in the cross-cultural aspects of nonverbal communication. He teaches in the Speech Department at California State University in Long Beach, California.

Prereading Questions

This article describes cross-cultural misunderstanding due to nonverbal behavior. What cross-cultural misunderstanding might arise in these situations?

1. an American customer waiting to be helped in a busy department store in Puerto Rico

   _____

   _____

   _____

   _____

2. an American businessman conducting a management seminar for Saudi Arabian corporate trainees

   _____

   _____

   _____

   _____

3. a white American school teacher reprimanding a black child

   _____

   _____

   _____

   _____

Nonverbal Behavior: Some Intricate and Diverse Dimensions in Intercultural Communication

John Smith has just returned to New York from a vacation in Puerto Rico. John told his friends that since he understood and spoke Spanish, he had no problems communicating with people over there. John also said that he wasn't surprised that the area was rather underdeveloped. "After all, people there have no sense of organization. Even their business behavior is quite disorganized," John said. "For instance, I once walked to a counter in one of the largest department stores in San Juan, the capital, around noon. The salesman was talking to a couple of native customers; however, as soon as I arrived, he greeted me and asked what he could do for me. I thanked him and told him to attend first to those he was already serving. The salesman smiled and continued the transaction with his customers. In the meantime, other people arrived, interrupted, were served, and left while I stood quietly fuming and waiting for my turn, which, incidentally, the salesman never acknowledged. I tell you these people don't have any sense of order or business." At the same time in Dammam, Saudi Arabia, Jim Ralph was flown from the U.S. head office to conduct a management seminar for the Saudi personnel in the branch of one of the largest corporations in the United States. In commenting on the seminar members to the North American branch manager, Jim said, "These people are strangely nervous and jerky. Every time I come close or talk to one of them, the man's body bolts up and tenses in his seat. I wonder what kind of managers they will be." While in Compton, California, white, Anglo-Saxon, Protestant Miss Mary Moore in her elementary school classroom was shouting angrily at little black Johnny: "For the hundredth time, you look at me and listen when I talk to you! Is that clear?" Johnny, meanwhile, looked up at her, down at the floor, turned and looked sideways while the teacher stood burning, helpless, and frustrated as she later told a friend.

In all of these examples there is a communication breakdown based primarily on misunderstanding and unawareness of the subtle cultural nonverbal cues in each context. John Smith, in Puerto Rico, though able to speak Spanish, when faced with a different concept of time reverted to his own cultural behavior patterns and found Puerto Ricans having no sense of order or business. John Smith, in that department store, misunderstood the interactional cycle of behavior in terms of the culture's perception of time. John Smith expected a monochronic pattern of interpersonal communication, where one customer at a time was attended to, and every customer was to be served in the order of his arrival. What happened was that John Smith was faced with a polychronic concept of time, where the salesman did not serve one customer at a time but rather tried to serve all customers at the same time. John Smith acted and reacted according to his North American cultural expectations: Time is structured in monochronic segments. Things are attended to one at a time. In this instance, customers should expect to be served in the order of their arrival or they are owed an apology or an explanation. Or, to be charitable, it is simply an inefficient and failing organization. On the other hand, from the salesman's cultural perspective he felt he had done his duty and was quite courteous. As soon as John Smith walked in, he was greeted and his presence was acknowledged while the transactions with other customers were continuing efficiently. John Smith, however, was quiet and seemed to want to wait, or maybe he wanted to look around for a while before he made up his mind. Anyway, he never mentioned what he wanted while many other customers arrived, were served, and left.

The salesman's behavior reflects a polychronic segmentation of time in interpersonal relations where interaction at several different levels is carried on simultaneously. The same behavior can be observed here for example, in Any Town, U.S.A., in ethnic Armenian, Greek, Lebanese, or Syrian grocery stores where we see the "foreign" salesperson trying to serve several customers simultaneously and regardless of the order of their arrival. In social or business interactions involving a North American and a Latin American or a Middle Easterner, or sometimes certain Southern Europeans, the North American may be talking or listening to the other party when the "foreigner" may "interrupt inappropriately" to acknowledge the presence of another individual. In no case is either party's business or social behavior inefficient, slighting, or insulting, or intended to frustrate, irritate, or aggravate. It is simply a different cultural structuring and meaning of temporal cycles in interpersonal interactions.

On the other hand, Jim Ralph's description of the behavior of his management trainees was quite accurate. His interpretation, however, was wrong. What Ralph viewed as nervous, jittery behavior was a native manifestation of attention, deference, and courtesy. Jim Ralph was regarded by the seminar members as the North American expert from overseas. He was a man accorded an especially distinguished and superior rank. Jim Ralph was in a status-conscious society whose members' interactions are marked by formalized rituals in which the nonverbal dimension is very important. Contexts involving superior-subordinate, instructor-student, or trainer-trainee interactions in the

85 Middle East, as in many traditional societies, are usually of a formal nature where role, status, and rank are clear and definite. In the Middle East, when a party of higher status or rank approaches or addresses another, the verbal response of the other party is usually preceded or accompanied by a reshuffling and a straightening of the body

90 posture whether one is standing or sitting. To a native that nonverbal message simply denotes respect, courtesy, and attention. In other words, what Jim Ralph saw according to his North American cultural perspective as peculiar nervous reflexes were conscious and deliberate native cultural nonverbal behaviors meant to convey messages

95 of deference and interest. They were intended by the Middle Eastern management trainees to improve an atmosphere for communication and understanding.

By the same token, in Compton (near Los Angeles), Mary Moore, the elementary school teacher, was in a strange and confusing

100 environment. As a dedicated and responsible teacher, she felt it her duty to straighten out impolite behaviors in her young charges in this almost all black school. Yet, at times, it seemed like a most frustrating, irritating, and exasperating task. She thinks the kids don't seem to listen to her. When she was talking to little black Johnny, from her

105 WASP (white, Anglo-Saxon, Protestant) perspective, the kid seemed listless, inattentive, and uninterested. On the other hand, Johnny was confused and helpless. He cast his eyes downward as a sign of respect when the teacher spoke to him, as a "good kid" should do according to his Mom and Dad at home, yet that seemed to infuriate

110 the teacher and make her shout at him. Both the teacher and the student in this instance were victims of conflicting cultural nonverbal behavior expectations that caused a communication breakdown. Mary Moore expected that with clear demonstrations of anger and admonition, Johnny's insolent manners or irresponsible nonverbal

115 behavior would adjust to "proper North American standards." In the meantime, Johnny expected that by behaving politely and casting his eyes downward when spoken to, Miss Moore would conform and respond according to the "proper North American standards" that he saw and heard about at home. The two "proper North American

120 standards" are obviously those of white middle-class America and black ghetto America, where nonverbal communication is often reflected and manifested in sets of different behaviors. In this case, little black Johnny sent a message of respect and attention, while Mary Moore from a WASP cultural perspective saw in the same

125 message insolence and inattention.

From Fathi Yousef, "Nonverbal Behavior: Some Intricate and Diverse Dimensions in Intercultural Communication."

Postreading Questions

1. The author, Fathi Yousef, uses some technical terms in this selection. They are important terms to use when talking about the subject of nonverbal behavior, and you may wish to use them yourself when you write or talk about this topic. Some of these words may be new to you and you may not have been sure of their meanings the first time you saw them. Fortunately, however, Yousef has used most of them in such a way that their meanings can be guessed from their contexts (the words around them).

   Look back at the selection and find the words and expressions in the following list. Try to guess their meanings by studying their contexts. Write your guesses, then check them by consulting your dictionary and your teacher.

   a. a monochronic pattern of interpersonal communication

   _____

   _____

   b. a polychronic concept of time _____

   _____

   _____

   c. superior-subordinate interaction _____

   _____

   _____

   d. cultural expectations _____

   _____

   _____

   e. a status-conscious society _____

   _____

   _____

   f. an *American* (*WASP*, *Middle Eastern*, etc.) cultural perspective _____

   _____

   _____

2. Outline the main ideas in the seletion by completing the following chart. Some items are only partially completed. Try to do this without looking back at Yousef's article.

Situation	Cultures	Social Setting	Problem	Issue	Cultural Perspective
Example:					
1		In a store		Percep-	United States:
				tion of	Wait on customers
				time and	one at a time
				order	and in order of
					their arrival
					Puerto Rico: Wait
					on all customers
					at the same time.
Example:					
2	United				
	States				
	and Saudi				
	Arabian				

Situation	Cultures	Social Setting	Problem	Issue	Cultural Perspective
Example:					
3	*WASP and*		*Teacher*		
	black		*angry*		
			at student;		
			student		
			confused		

3. From your experience and knowledge, is the author's explanation of the cross-cultural behavior and subsequent misunderstanding in *these particular situations* accurate? Explain your answer. Have any of the experiences or situations described by Yousef ever happened to you? What happened? Supply *other* examples of cross-cultural misunderstanding that could arise in the situations described by Yousef.

Gathering Information

By doing one or all of the following exercises, you'll get a chance to learn even more about nonverbal behavior in your own culture and in other cultures.

1. With your classmates, think of examples of nonverbal behavior from various cultures in addition to those already presented. Take notes and organize your information in the following chart. Look for examples of nonverbal behavior in these areas:

   a. gestures and facial expressions
   b. how people use and perceive time
   c. how people use and perceive space

Culture	Nonverbal Behavior	Meaning

2. Choose an example of nonverbal behavior and find out what it means in three different cultures. Interview your classmates, Americans, other foreigners in your community, or people from your own culture. Take notes and organize your information in the following chart.

Nonverbal Behavior	Meaning: Culture 1	Meaning: Culture 2	Meaning: Culture 3

3. Watch at least one half hour of an American television program or movie. Turn the sound down. Make a list of as many examples of nonverbal behavior as you can. Indicate what you think each one means. Record your information in the following chart and share it with your classmates. Note: Soap operas, situation comedies, and dramatic/action programs are best suited to this exercise.

Title of Program or Film	Date and Time	Nonverbal Behavior	Possible Meaning
Example:			
M.A.S.H.	November 2, 7:00 pm	Man scratches head and raises eyebrows	Is confused

PART TWO

LANGUAGE FOR WRITING

INTERPRETING NONVERBAL BEHAVIOR

In his article on nonverbal behavior, Fathi Yousef *explains* or *interprets* some cross-cultural examples of nonverbal behavior. In doing so, he uses certain words and phrases that express his observations and his interpretation of what he has observed. This kind of language is useful in all academic writing, including the social sciences, such as anthropology and psychology. It is also useful in writing in fields such as physics, chemistry, and biology.

Some of the expressions Yousef uses are in the following list. Find them in their original contexts in the article first and study their meanings and how they are used in sentences. Also, notice the underlined verb endings. Then copy the contexts in the space provided. The first one is done for you; you find the rest. When you've finished, do the exercise that follows.

1. the/this behavior reflect<u>s</u> . . . (a cultural value)

   The salesman's behavior reflects a polychronic segmentation of time in interpersonal relations. . . .

   _____

   _____

2. the/this behavior can be/is observ<u>ed</u> + *place* (or "in American culture")

   _____

   _____

   _____

3. the/this behavior is a manifestation of + *abstract noun* (a cultural value)

   _____

   _____

   _____

4. the/this behavior denote<u>s</u> + *abstract noun* (a cultural value)

   _____

   _____

   _____

5. the/this behavior convey<u>s</u> messages of *abstract noun* (a cultural value)

   _____

   _____

   _____

Here are some additional expressions to use when interpreting and observing behavior:

6. the/this behavior can be interpret<u>ed</u> as . . .

7. the/this behavior show<u>s</u> + . . .

8. the/this behavior mean<u>s</u> + *that* . . .

9. the/this behavior is consider<u>ed</u> to be . . .

10. the/this behavior is associat<u>ed</u> with . . .

What other nouns could substitute for the word *behavior* in the preceding expressions (for example, *action, gesture, facial expression, movement, attitude,* and so forth)?

Practicing What You've Learned

Using the information you gathered in Part One, either draw five to ten pictures or diagrams of different examples of nonverbal behavior from your culture or any other or find pictures of them in magazines, newspapers, or photographs. Next to each picture, write a sentence *interpreting* the behavior. Use each of the preceding expressions at least once.

PART THREE
SYSTEMS FOR WRITING
ESSAY ORGANIZATION

In previous chapters, you have seen techniques for organizing paragraphs so that the reader can easily follow your ideas. In an essay, too, there are techniques for establishing order, and these techniques are essential for maintaining a good relationship with your reader.

The key to essay organization is in your thesis statement. First of all, think of your thesis statement as a mini-outline for your entire essay. It's like a map the reader studies before embarking on the voyage on which your essay will take him. It not only tells the reader where he's going, but also how he's going to get there. Therefore, a good thesis statement tells the reader what you are going to talk about and how you are going to organize your ideas. As you saw in Chapter 9, a good thesis statement consists of a main idea and the ideas that support the main idea.

Read the following thesis statement:

It is extremely important to be aware of the cross-cultural differences in nonverbal behavior in order to avoid misunderstanding, develop a deeper appreciation of other cultures, and communicate effectively.

What is the main idea? What are the supporting ideas? How will the essay be organized? Finish the following outline to show the probable organization of an essay beginning with this thesis statement.

First paragraph: Introduction, including thesis statement

Second paragraph: _____

_____

Third paragraph: _____

_____

Fourth paragraph: _____

_____

Fifth paragraph: Conclusion

There are many ways to organize an essay. The organization system you just saw is one you can use for any expository essay. The following are organization systems for essays with specific purposes. More organizational patterns can be made by combining the different types outlined here. As you progress in your writing, you will learn many new ways to organize your thoughts in an essay.

System A: Showing Cause and Effect

First paragraph: There are three causes/effects of X: a, b, and c.
Second paragraph: All about x and a
Third paragraph: All about x and b
Fourth paragraph: All about x and c
Fifth paragraph: Conclusion

System B: Comparing Two Things

First paragraph: X is similar to (different from) Y in three areas: a, b, and c.

Second paragraph: All about x and y in light of a

Third paragraph: All about x and y in light of d

Fourth paragraph: All about x and y in light of c

Fifth paragraph: Conclusion

System C: Showing Advantages and/or Disadvantages

First paragraph: X has three (dis)advantages: 1, 2, and 3.
Second paragraph: All about first (dis)advantage
Third paragraph: All about second (dis)advantage
Fourth paragraph: All about third (dis)advantage
Fifth paragraph: Conclusion

Remember, the thesis statement tells the reader where the writer is going and how he or she is going to get there. Writers *usually* use the systems described in this section when they are explaining something (exposition), showing cause and effect, comparing, or discussing advantages and disadvantages. Sometimes, however, the topic of an essay requires the writer to compare *and* show cause and effect, or to combine any two or three (or more) of the systems. In this case, the essay may contain one paragraph devoted to cause and effect and another to comparison. In other words, you can combine parts of these system types, just as long as your thesis statement prepares the reader for the essay to follow.

Practicing What You've Learned

Exercise 1 Read the following thesis statements and describe how you think the essays they introduce are going to be organized. First, decide what the main idea is and then determine the supporting points. Take note of the *order* in which the supporting ideas are presented. Then, make outlines like the preceding ones to show the possible organization of an essay.

1. The gestures people use in the United States or Canada when greeting family members, insulting others, and showing respect for superiors are different from those used in the Middle East.

    _____

    _____

    _____

    _____

    _____

    _____

    _____

    _____

    _____

2. Learning to write has influenced me in three ways: I think more clearly, I have more self-discipline, and I am able to concentrate better.

    _____

    _____

    _____

    _____

    _____

_____

_____

_____

_____

_____

3. There are three advantages to the traditional grading system: It motivates students to work harder, it provides a standardized measure of student achievement, and it is objective rather than subjective.

_____

_____

_____

_____

_____

_____

_____

_____

4. Although they are very different, both physical and mental leisure-time activities have benefits that are stimulating and constructive.

_____

_____

_____

_____

_____

_____

_____

_____

_____

_____

5. Both travel and study in a foreign country result in intellectual and emotional growth.

_____

_____

_____

_____

_____

_____

_____

6. It is important to learn the nonverbal language of a new culture in order to communicate effectively in that culture and to have a complete understanding of it.

_____

_____

_____

_____

_____

_____

_____

_____

_____

Exercise 2   Your teacher is going to assign one of the essays in the following "Assignments" section (or ask you to choose one). Before you actually start to write, do the following exercise. Follow these steps:

Step 1:   Study the essay assignment carefully, then write your thesis statement for it. Follow the brainstorming guidelines in Chapter 9.

Step 2:   _Before_ you write the essay itself, exchange your thesis statement with a partner and see if you can determine an organizational pattern for him or her, based solely on the thesis statement. If this is too difficult, the thesis probably isn't complete enough. Rewrite it. If it's easy, congratulations—you probably have a good thesis.

Step 3: If your thesis checks out with your partner, take it back and on the same piece of paper briefly outline the essay you intend to write. The outline should include your thesis, the topic sentences of all of your paragraphs, and brief descriptions of the examples you intend to use to develop each paragraph. See the example below:

First paragraph: Thesis statement

Second paragraph: Topic sentence of the first paragraph of the body

Example 1 _____

Example 2 _____

etc.

Third paragraph: Topic sentence of the second paragraph of the body

Examples _____

_____

_____

Fourth paragraph: Topic sentence of the third paragraph of the body

Examples _____

_____

_____

Step 4: Give the thesis and outline to your teacher and have him or her check your organization and ideas at this point, to see if you're on the right track. Your teacher may ask you to start over or may tell you to go ahead and write your first draft.

Assignments

1. Show the differences or similarities in nonverbal behavior in two cultures. You can compare your own culture with U.S./Canadian culture, or you can choose any two cultures that interest you.

2. Show how nonverbal behavior can cause cross-cultural misunderstanding.

3. Describe and illustrate three examples of cross-cultural behavior in a particular culture. Be sure to explain the behavior in terms of the cultural values it represents. You can discuss nonverbal behavior in your culture or any other.

4. Illustrate the nonverbal aspects of a particular function in three different cultures. You may wish to choose one of the following:
   - greeting a friend of the same sex
   - greeting a friend of the opposite sex
   - showing respect
   - greeting a stranger
   - insulting someone

5. Agree with, disagree with, or explain the following quotation:

   "Probably no more than thirty to thirty-five percent of the social meaning of a conversation or interaction is carried by the words."—Ray Birdwhistell, American anthropologist

PART FOUR

EVALUATING FOR REWRITING

Working with Your Partner

Exchange essays with your partner and answer the following questions about your partner's paper.

1. Before you actually read the essay, locate the thesis statement and write it here:

   _____

   _____

   _____

   _____

   Answer the following questions based on your understanding of the thesis statement.

2. What is the main idea?

   _____

   _____

   _____

   _____

3. What are the supporting ideas? List them in the order in which they appear in the thesis.

   _____

   _____

   _____

   _____

   _____

4. Which organizational system do you think the essay will follow (expository, cause and effect, comparison, advantages and disadvantages, or a combination)?

   _____

5. Now, fill in the following outline to show the probable organization of the essay.

   First paragraph: _____

   _____

   Second paragraph: _____

   _____

   Third paragraph: _____

   _____

   _____

   Fourth paragraph: _____

   _____

   Fifth paragraph: _____

   _____

6. Now, read the entire essay. Were your predictions accurate?

   Yes _____   No _____

7. If the answer to Question 6 was *no*, briefly explain how the author can rewrite the thesis statement to present a clearer "map" for the reader. Also, mention any changes required within the essay itself.

   _____

   _____

   _____

   _____

_____
_____
_____
_____

8. Now, rate the essay, keeping in mind all the material you've learned in this chapter as well as in previous chapters.

Rating	The essay . . .
1	needs major revisions.
2	is good in parts, but the thesis sentence and/or the overall organization is unclear.
3	is very good; the thesis is clear, the organization is easy to follow, and the ideas are well developed.

Working on Your Own

Now you should be ready to evaluate your own paper. Go through the questions again. Take into consideration what your partner said about your essay when she or he evaluated it. Are there unclear elements? Is anything missing? Is there more to say? Words to change? Finally, score your own paragraph before you turn it in to the teacher. Did you earn a 3 this time?

CHAPTER 11
TECHNOLOGY

Laser spectroscopy.

1. Robotic automobile assembly.

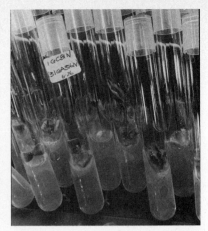

2. Genetic engineering of crop plants.

3. Nuclear power plant cooling towers.

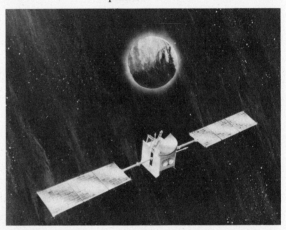

4. Artist rendition of a communication satellite.

5. Using computer graphics to study the human heart.

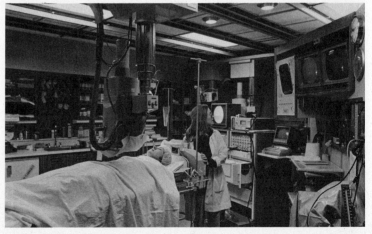

6. A sophisticated medical diagnostic scan.

PART ONE

IDEAS FOR WRITING

TECHNOLOGICAL INNOVATIONS

How has your life been influenced by high technology? What examples of advanced technology are around you every day? Look around you now. How has advanced technology contributed to what you see? Now look at the pictures on the left, which illustrate some examples of advanced technology. With a partner, tell what each one shows. Have you personally seen scenes like these? If so, where?

Brainstorming

Now for each of the images, think of advantages and disadvantages of the technology they illustrate. List these in the following chart and add more examples if you can. Compare notes with your partner.

Example	Advantages	Disadvantages
Robotics	Gets boring or dangerous work done faster. Creates technical and engineering jobs.	Eliminates certain kinds of jobs.
_____	_____	_____
_____	_____	_____
_____	_____	_____
_____	_____	_____
_____	_____	_____
_____	_____	_____
_____	_____	_____
_____	_____	_____

Freewriting

Some people believe that through technology the world has become a safer and more comfortable place. Others believe that technology has taken people away from their natural environment and is dehumanizing. How do *you* feel about technology? Do the advantages outweigh the disadvantages? Write for twenty minutes without stopping about the advantages and/or disadvantages of technology. Include specific technological innovations if possible.

Reading for Ideas

Prereading Questions

1. What documents did you need in order to come to the United States or Canada?

2. For international students, the most important piece of identification is often their passport. Take a look at your passport and answer the following questions.

   a. Where was your passport issued?
   b. How big is it? Can it fit in your pocket?
   c. How long did it take you to apply for and receive your passport? Describe the application process.
   d. What information does your passport contain?
   e. Would it be easy to alter information on your passport?
   f. Did you have a long wait to pass through customs when you first arrived here? What did the customs official do? How long did it take him or her to read your passport?

Now read the following newspaper article, which describes how technology is changing U.S. passports.

U.S. Passports Changing with Technology

The United States is issuing a new, machine-readable passport intended to speed the passage of travelers across international boundaries.

The new passport is smaller, easier to carry and use, and easier to manufacture. And it is harder to counterfeit or alter, which should help officials intercept fugitives or locate persons needed in emergencies. 5

So far, the new document is being issued only by the U.S. passport agencies in Washington and Chicago. Los Angeles is scheduled to

10 start early next year, with other U.S. passport agencies following in the next few years.

A person receiving the new type of passport also gets a notice from the State Department saying, "Your new machine-readable passport is a historic U.S. government document."

15 "It is one of the first passports to be issued under automated technology," the notice says, "and marks a major breakthrough by the Department of State in more efficient and economical service to the United States' international traveling public."

The passport is unprecedented in several ways. As usual, the
20 document lists the holder's name, sex, birthdate, place of birth, and the passport's number and expiration date—all printed out for anyone to read. But it also lists the same data on two lines of letters and figures resembling the account numbers printed on checks of commercial banks.

25 When the new system is in operation, Americans leaving or entering the United States will present their passport at the border, where an official will pass the document through a machine that will optically read the coded data in a moment—and signal an alarm if the holder is a fugitive or wanted for some emergency, such as a death in the
30 family.

Such a system was adopted by the International Civil Aviation Organization, which started developing the plan in 1968 when a big increase in international air travel on huge aircraft began to swamp border control officers with surges of passengers all wanting imme-
35 diate attention.

Most U.S. border control officers now read passports visually and check the names manually in a "watch" book as thick as a Manhattan telephone directory. This can cause massive delays or tempt the control officers not to check every name.

40 Countries with heavy international passenger traffic have agreed to use the machine-readable passports, but only the United States has started issuing them. Programs in Great Britain, West Germany, and other European countries have bogged down for various reasons.

45 Even the United States has only half a system—it hasn't installed the machines to read the passports at the border.

Because U.S. passports are good for five years, it will take at least that long to get all U.S. passport bearers under the new system.

Connecting the reading machines to computers raises possibilities
50 for storing all kinds of records of individuals' international travel. But officials say they have no intention of keeping track of travel by Americans. They say they want to use the process merely to speed

the check against names in the "watch" book. The data on U.S. passports is kept at a minimum.

Other countries are debating whether to list national identity 55 numbers or other information. The international agreement on machine-readable passports prohibits inclusion of any secret data in the coding.

As finally approved by international agreement, the code must be readable to the naked eye as well as to machines, primarily to protect 60 the holder against violation of his secrecy rights. Still, some persons are going to be suspicious.

Precautions against fraud have been worked into the new passports. The laminated plastic that covers the picture and information on the data page appears to be transparent, but when examined under 65 the glare of a flashlight displays the American eagle and shield as in a watermark—a hard thing for a counterfeiter to duplicate. The new laminate is pressed on by a machine instead of by someone using an electric iron in the method traditional around the world.

James E. Roper, Newhouse News Service, Robert G. Fichenberg, bureau chief

Postreading Questions

Make a list of as many advantages and disadvantages of the new passport as you can think of and find in the article.

Advantages   **Disadvantages**

_____   _____

_____   _____

_____   _____

_____   _____

_____   _____

_____   _____

_____   _____

_____   _____

_____   _____

_____   _____

Advantages	Disadvantages	PART TWO
_____	_____	
_____	_____	
_____	_____	

Gathering Information

Technological innovations have improved human life but have also had negative effects. In the interest of finding advantages as well as disadvantages of technology, do some research on *one* of the following issues. Locate the *Readers' Guide to Periodicals* in the library. Choose an issue and look up the topic(s) (given in parentheses in the following list) in a recent copy of a magazine or journal. Make a chart similar to the one you did in "Brainstorming" to list advantages and disadvantages. Share your results with your classmates.

1. Using computers as teaching machines (technology, computers, computer assisted instruction, education)
2. Robots as workers (robotics, technology)
3. Eliminating congenital diseases through genetic engineering (genetic engineering)
4. Generating electricity through nuclear power (nuclear power)
5. Investigating life in space or on another planet (space exploration)
6. Arresting the growth of cancer cells through radiation therapy (radiation therapy)

Hold a debate in which you discuss the advantages and disadvantages of one aspect of technology. Follow the debate guidelines presented in Chapter 8.

PART TWO

LANGUAGE FOR WRITING

CITING AUTHORITIES

In addition to giving clear explanations and using examples, you can support your ideas by referring to the work and ideas of others; this is called *citing authorities*. When you use someone else's exact words, all the words *must* be placed within quotation marks ("...") and the author must be cited.

Go back to the article "U.S. Passports Changing with Technology." Reread it quickly and look for the quoted passage that begins in the fourth paragraph.

1. Who/what is the source? Who said (or wrote) the quoted passage?

   _____

   _____

2. Does the quotation support the main idea of the article?

   Yes _____   No _____

3. Why do you think Roper chose to quote this particular passage?

   _____

   _____

   _____

Here are three common ways of incorporating quotations into your writing:

1. According to [author] in [source], "...."

   Example: According to James E. Roper in "U.S. Passports Changing with Technology," the new machine-readable passport is "unprecedented in several ways."

2. According to [source] by [author], "...."

   Example: According to an article by James E. Roper, the new passport is difficult to "counterfeit or alter, which should help officials intercept fugitives or locate persons needed in emergencies."

3. In [source], [author] says (said, states) "...."

   Example: In "U.S. Passports Changing with Technology," James E. Roper states that programs to implement the new passports in European countries "have bogged down for various reasons" and that even in the United States it will take at least five years to distribute the new passports to American applicants.

Be careful not to overuse quotations. Use a quotation only when the author's own words have a high degree of impact or cannot be improved on. Use the author's first and last name or only the last name. Do not use the author's first name alone. Underline book titles and the names of newspapers and magazines. Put quotation marks around the titles of articles.

Practicing What You've Learned

Refer to your chart in Part One showing the advantages and disadvantages of the new passports. Using the information in your chart, write five to ten sentences describing either advantages or disadvantages. Incorporate all or part of the following quotations from the article and refer to one of the preceding formulas.

1. "The United States is issuing a new, machine-readable passport intended to speed the passage of travelers across international boundaries."

2. "Connecting the reading machines to computers raises possibilities for storing all kinds of records of individuals' international travel."

3. "The new passport is smaller, easier to carry and use, and easier to manufacture."

4. "Countries with heavy international passenger traffic have agreed to use the machine-readable passports, but only the United States has started issuing them. Programs in Great Britain, West Germany, and other European countries have bogged down for various reasons."

PARAPHRASING

A second way to support your ideas by referring to sources is to *paraphrase* a relevant part of the article and explain how it supports your topic sentence. A paraphrase is a restatement of a phrase or sentence that is approximately as long as the original statement. A paraphrase is used when *restating* the author's words is both more efficient and effective. Citing the source is still necessary. Although a paraphrase should be, for the most part, your *own* words, it is correct occasionally to use the author's exact words if he or she has used specialized or technical terminology for which there is no adequate synonym. Note the following examples:

Quotation: "Genetic engineering on plants will produce 'super crops' by the year 2000, including square tomatoes for easy packing and short corn stalks loaded with ears."

Source: A study done by L. William Teweles & Co.

Paraphrase: A study conducted by L. William Teweles & Co. predicts that genetic engineering will produce superior food crops such as square tomatoes by the year 2000.

Notice that some of the language from the original quotation was repeated ("genetic engineering"—there's only one term for this—and "produce"—there's no adequate synonym for it in this context), but the paraphrase is clearly not the words of the study by L. William Teweles & Co. Notice also that the corn example was not included. In developing an idea, if you have a need for a concrete detail and your original source contains one, use it. If you want to save space or time by using a paraphrase, you can do so by omitting some of the details the source may contain.

Here's a helpful hint: Sometimes it is useful to look up in the dictionary the words in a quotation that you don't know. You have to understand the meaning of a word before you can paraphrase it. A thesaurus (dictionary of synonyms) is also useful when paraphrasing.

Practicing What You've Learned

Exercise 1   Write paraphrases for the following quotations about issues in advanced technology. Refer to the preceding guidelines. *Don't forget to cite the sources.*

1. *Quotation:* "Routine, repetitive, and dreary blue-collar materials-handling jobs are going to be filled by robots for less than the minimum hourly wage."
   Source: The Copely News Service

2. *Quotation:* "A new program at the Defense Advanced Research Projects Agency (DARPA) will develop computers capable of symbolic reasoning with effective computational speeds 1,000 times greater than those used in military systems today."
   Source: Robert Cooper, Director of DARPA (Note: Figures are like technical terminology—you can't paraphrase them.)

3. *Quotation:* "The Japanese aim to produce machines easy enough to use, and intelligent and fast enough in their responses, to come close to the kinds of transactions intelligent human beings are used to having with each other."
   Source: The Fifth Generation, by Edward Feigenbaum and Pamela McCorduck (Note: This is a book about the supercomputers being developed in Japan.)

Exercise 2   Write a paragraph in which you discuss one advantage or disadvantage of a particular technical advancement. Use one quotation and at least one paraphrase. Base your writing on the ideas and sources from your research in Part One.

PART THREE

SYSTEMS FOR WRITING

ESSAY DEVELOPMENT

In Chapter 10, you learned how to organize an essay and you saw the similarities in organization between paragraphs and essays. The *development* of an essay is also closely related to the development of a paragraph. In Chapter 4, you learned that adequate paragraph development is the result of using concrete, precise words, appropriate transitions, and explanations that fully explain the ideas. A well-developed essay has concrete, relevant details, transitions between paragraphs, and logically developed ideas that support the topic sentences and the thesis statement. The paragraphs should be balanced; they should have the same degree of depth, impact, and length.

Read the following essay about a technological development and then answer the questions.

At the present time, there is a great deal of interest in the use of computers in education. The educational use of computers is called Computer Assisted Instruction, or CAI. Many public schools in the United States have acquired computers and CAI programs to run on them. School districts are establishing computer resource centers and special training programs to help teachers use computers. In addition, some colleges and universities are beginning to establish "computer literacy" requirements for graduation. In spite of all this interest in the use of computers in education, some educators and students still may be wondering if this expensive toy is really worth their time and, in some cases, money. The answer is a definite *yes:* The use of computers in education has important benefits for both students and teachers.

Computers enhance a student's learning experience in many ways. First of all, the computer has the ability to accommodate individual differences in learning speed because the user (the student) is the one who controls the pace of the lessons. In addition, because a computer is nonjudgmental, the learner does not have to be afraid of reprisal or humiliation when making errors. For example, because computers can repeat information over and over, the user can ask for many repetitions of a lesson without fearing a judgmental response about his or her ability to learn. The beneficial effects of learning in a stress-free atmosphere are well documented. Another advantage of CAI is that a computer can give a student immediate feedback. It can tell the student why he or she is wrong as soon as an error is made, and it can even provide an appropriate hint as to how to figure out what the correct answer is.

Not only do computers benefit students, they also make the teacher's job easier. One advantage lies in the preparation of instructional materials. Schools and colleges can purchase educational computer programs that can be adapted to any learning situation. These systems, called "authoring systems," are like skeletal lesson plans: The format of several exercises and tests is already planned out; all the teacher adds is the information he or she wants the students to learn (mathematical problems, vocabulary lists, and so forth). The authoring system automatically incorporates these teaching points into its preplanned format and then is ready to be used by several students for a long time. The system can also correct the students' work and determine and record grades. In addition, the computer offers numerous advantages to teachers in managing their classrooms. A computer laboratory (a room having one computer for every two students) can free the teacher to meet individually with students while the rest of the class is occupied with computer lessons. Finally, computers can help teachers keep student records and chart student progress, thereby cutting down on time-consuming paperwork.

With all of these advantages for both teachers and students, it is easy to see why there is so much interest in using computers in education. Of course, there are those who are skeptical and view computers as a passing fad. There are those also who simply are afraid of them. In time, however, computers will become as familiar in the classroom as chalkboards are today.

1. Look at the thesis statement. On the basis of this, what do you expect to read about in the essay? How do you expect the essay to be organized?

2. What are the supporting ideas in the thesis? Write them here:

_____

_____

_____

Are they balanced? That is, are they equally important?

Yes _____   No _____

3. Now review the rest of the essay. How does the writer move from one paragraph to another? Are the transitions between paragraphs smooth?

4. Make a list of details the writer includes in the paragraphs of the body.

_____

_____

_____

_____

_____

Are they concrete?   Are they relevant?

Yes _____   No _____   Yes _____   No _____

5. Are the paragraphs of the body logically developed?

Yes _____   No _____

Do they support the thesis statement?

Yes _____   No _____

Practicing What You've Learned

Exercise 1 The following essay discusses advantages and disadvantages of technology in general. However, it lacks details and paragraph transitions. Rewrite it so that it conforms to the description of a well-developed essay.

Technology is around us every day. We see examples of advanced technology at work, at home, in the city, and even in the country. Although technology has brought us many useful things, such as improved living conditions, it has also brought us disadvantages, such as air pollution.

As a result of technological innovation, our living conditions have improved dramatically. . . .

Air pollution is one of the negative results of advanced technology. . . .

Hint: Correct the thesis statement first.

Exercise 2 Brainstorming before starting an essay is the best way to generate specific, concrete, and relevant details to develop your ideas in writing. Refer to the brainstorming guidelines in Part Three of Chapter 9. As a class or in groups, choose one of the following assignments and brainstorm for ideas. Take notes, then write the essay on your own.

Assignments

1. Discuss the advantages and/or disadvantages of one aspect of advanced technology. You can choose one of the examples of advanced technology from the following list or think of one on your own.
   - military/weapons technology
   - the personal computer
   - nuclear energy
   - bioengineering (as it relates to agriculture or genetics)
   - Computer Assisted Instruction
   - robotics

2. Discuss the causes or effects of a technological advancement. Use the preceding list for examples.

3. Discuss the impact of one technological advancement on your home country or city.

4. Write an essay in answer to the following question: In general, has technology done more harm than good?

5. Respond to the following quotation: "In these days of urban decay and energy crisis, there is a constant longing to return to the land and flee back to a simpler way of life. But it can't be done."—Isaac Asimov

PART FOUR

EVALUATING FOR REWRITING

Working with Your Partner

Evaluate your partner's essay by answering the following questions.

1. Read only the first paragraph. Locate the thesis statement. On the basis of your understanding of the thesis, what do you expect to read about in the essay? How do you expect the essay to be organized? Explain briefly in the following space:

_____

_____

_____

_____

_____

_____

2. What are the supporting ideas in the thesis statement? Write them here:

_____

_____

_____

_____

_____

Are they balanced? That is, are they equally important?

Yes _____   No _____

If the answer is _no_, make suggestions for improvement.

_____

_____

_____

_____

_____

3. Now read the rest of the essay. How does the writer move from one paragraph to another? Are the transitions between paragraphs smooth? Explain.

_____

_____

_____

_____

_____

4. Make a list of details the writer includes in the body of the essay.

_____   _____

_____   _____

_____   _____

_____   _____

_____   _____

Are they concrete?

Yes _____ No _____

If the answer is *no,* make suggestions for improvement.

_____

_____

_____

_____

_____

_____

_____

Are the supporting ideas relevant?

Yes _____ No _____

If the answer is *no,* make suggestions for improvement.

_____

_____

_____

_____

_____

_____

_____

5. Are the paragraphs of the body logically developed? Do they support the thesis statement?

Yes _____ No _____

If the answer is *no,* how can the writer revise the body of the essay?

_____

_____

_____

_____

_____

_____

_____

6. Now, rate the entire essay, keeping in mind all the material you've learned in this chapter, as well as in previous chapters.

Rating	The essay . . .
1	needs major revisions.
2	is good in parts, but the thesis statement and/or the overall organization is unclear.
3	is very good; the thesis is clear, the organization is easy to follow, and the ideas are well developed.

Working on Your Own

Now you should be ready to evaluate your own essay. Go through the questions again. Take into consideration what your partner said about your essay development when he or she evaluated it. Are your supporting ideas balanced? Are the paragraphs of the body adequately developed? Is anything missing? Finally, score your own essay before you turn it in to the teacher. Did you earn a 3?

CHAPTER 12
LIVING TOGETHER ON A SMALL PLANET

Taking an I.Q. test.

PART ONE

IDEAS FOR WRITING

WHAT IS INTELLIGENCE?

If someone were to ask you "What is intelligence?" how would you answer? Would you say that an intelligent person has a high IQ, or gets good grades, or doesn't have to study? Whom do you consider to be intelligent? Think about your definition of intelligence for a moment. Is the definition determined by one's culture? How do we use intelligence in our everyday lives? Have we used our intelligence to create the world we live in? Think of examples that show how humans have or have not applied their intelligence. Discuss the answers to all of these questions with one or two classmates and then read the following definitions of intelligence.

1. "Intelligence is the ability to process information in such a way that it is useful in your life. There's a difference between intelligence and competence. The intelligent person is more flexible. He can apply his knowledge and abilities. For example, one can learn how to fix a car engine, but an intelligent person can apply those concepts to another type of engine. An intelligent person can extrapolate to another field."—Lucia Blakeslee

2. "Intelligence is the ability to grasp new information quickly and put it to use efficiently."—Nancy Vankat

3. "Intelligence is the capacity to do well on an intelligence test."—Edwin Boring

4. "Intelligence unites us with mankind, by leading us in sympathy to other times, other places, other customs."—John Erskine

5. "If an animal does something, they call it instinct. If we do exactly the same thing for the same reason, they call it intelligence. I guess what they mean is that we all make mistakes, but intelligence enables us to do it on purpose."—Will Cuppy

6. "Intellect distinguishes between the possible and the impossible; reason distinguishes between the sensible and the senseless. Even the possible can be senseless."—Max Born

Brainstorming

Some of the definitions in the previous section may have included language that is new to you. This exercise will help you understand this language in the context of defining intelligence, so that you can also use it in your writing and speaking.

The following is a list of some useful words and expressions. Make sure you understand each one, then supply an accurate synonym or synonymous expression for each in the following chart. Be sure to find synonyms that fit into the *context* of the topic of intelligence; to do this, go back and examine how the words and expressions listed are used in the sentences. At the end of the chart (p. 242), write any additional words or expressions that you find useful in discussing intelligence. Two are already listed.

Words and Expressions	Synonyms
to grasp new information	_____
	_____
to process information	_____
	_____
to do something on purpose	_____
	_____
to extrapolate	_____
	_____
the possible, the impossible, the sensible, etc.	_____
	_____
competence	_____
	_____
instinct	_____
	_____
reason	_____
	_____
capacity	_____
	_____
intellect	_____
	_____

Words and Expressions	Synonyms
IQ	
heredity	

Freewriting

What do *you* think intelligence is? Do you agree with any of the definitions in the previous section? Or do you have a completely different definition? Write for fifteen minutes on your personal definition of intelligence. As you write, consider the questions you discussed with your classmates at the beginning of this chapter.

Reading for Ideas

You are going to read a short essay on intelligence by Isaac Asimov. Asimov is a well-known American scientist who is also a prodigious author. He has written many works of science fiction, as well as factual articles and essays on science. Before you read "What Is Intelligence, Anyway?" answer the questions that precede the essay.

Prereading Questions

1. In your opinion, is there a relationship between *education* and *intelligence?* Explain.
2. Are there different *kinds* of intelligence? Explain.
3. Can intelligence be measured? How?
4. What do you know about intelligence tests? Have you ever taken one? What are the advantages and disadvantages of intelligence tests?
5. Are there cultural differences in the way we define intelligence? Explain.

What Is Intelligence, Anyway?

What is intelligence, anyway? When I was in the army I received a kind of aptitude test that all soldiers took and, against a normal of 100, I scored 160. No one at the base had ever seen a figure like that, and for two hours they made a big fuss over me. (It didn't
5   mean anything. The next day I was still a buck private with KP as my highest duty.)

All my life I've been registering scores like that, so that I have the complacent feeling that I'm highly intelligent, and I expect other people to think so, too. Actually, though, don't such scores simply
10   mean that I am very good at answering the type of academic questions that are considered worthy of answers by the people who make up the intelligence tests—people with intellectual bents similar to mine?

For instance, I had an auto-repair man once, who, on these
15   intelligence tests, could not possibly have scored more than 80, by my estimate. I always took it for granted that I was far more intelligent than he was. Yet, when anything went wrong with my car, I hastened to him with it, watched him anxiously as he explored its vitals, and listened to his pronouncements as though they were divine oracles—
20   and he always fixed my car.

Well, then, suppose my auto-repair man devised questions for an intelligence test. Or suppose a carpenter did, or a farmer, or, indeed, almost anyone but an academician. By every one of those tests, I'd prove myself a moron. And I'd *be* a moron, too. In a world where I
25   could not use my academic training and my verbal talents but had to do something intricate or hard, working with my hands, I would do poorly. My intelligence, then, is not absolute, but is a function of the society I live in and of the fact that a small subsection of that society has managed to foist itself on the rest as an arbiter of such matters. foist: push
30   Consider my auto-repair man, again. He had a habit of telling me jokes whenever he saw me. One time he raised his head from under the automobile hood to say: ''Doc, a deaf-and-dumb guy went into a hardware store to ask for some nails. He put two fingers together on the counter and made hammering motions with the other hand.
35   The clerk brought him a hammer. He shook his head and pointed to the two fingers he was hammering. The clerk brought him nails. He picked out the sizes he wanted, and left. Well, doc, the next guy who came in was a blind man. He wanted scissors. How do you suppose he asked for them?''
40   Indulgently, I lifted my right hand and made scissoring motions with

my first two fingers. Whereupon my auto-repair man laughed raucously and said, "Why, you dumb jerk, he used his *voice* and asked for them." Then he said, smugly, "I've been trying that on all my customers today." "Did you catch many?" I asked. "Quite a few," he said, "but I knew for sure I'd catch *you*." "Why is that?" I asked. "Because you're so goddamned educated, doc, I *knew* you couldn't be very smart."   He's so intelligent that he couldn't

And I have an uneasy feeling he had something there.   be very smart.

Isaac Asimov

Postreading Questions

1. What was the reaction to Asimov's score on the army aptitude test he took? Did his score affect his status in the army? Find support in the article for your answers.

_____

_____

_____

_____

_____

_____

2. What does Asmiov think the *real* meaning of a high score on an intelligence test is? Refer to the words in the article that support your answer.

_____

_____

_____

_____

_____

3. How would Asimov do on a test designed by an electrician? Where in the text does he state this?

_____

_____

_____

_____

_____

4. Find the part of Asimov's essay in which he defines intelligence; paraphrase his definition.

_____

_____

_____

_____

_____

5. Why does Asimov relate the auto repairman's joke? How does this support Asimov's thesis?

_____

_____

_____

Gathering Information

Whom do you consider to be very intelligent? Choose a well-known figure (past or present) famous for brilliant thinking and find out as much as you can about why this person is considered intelligent. Do his or her qualities match any of those described by the definitions in the first section? Choose someone from any field, in any country. You might choose a philosopher, a scientist, a writer, a teacher, an inventor, or a mechanic! Write a paragraph on why this person is considered intelligent.

PART TWO

LANGUAGE FOR WRITING

SUMMARIZING

A summary is a kind of report on something that someone else already has written. It is usually shorter than the original material, but it contains all of the important points of the original. This is because the purpose of a summary is to *save time and space*. Therefore, in writing a summary, you have to *condense* information.

A summary is like a paraphrase in that you are expressing someone else's ideas in your own words and you are giving credit to the original author. It is unlike a paraphrase in that it is taken from a larger body of work. A paraphrase comes from an idea or two, or a sentence or two, that someone else has originated. A summary, however, can be derived from an article, a chapter of a book, or even an entire book. In summarizing something, you often have to restate the author's original ideas; therefore, paraphrasing is part of summarizing.

In academic courses, you often will be asked to write summaries. Professors sometimes ask students to summarize articles or books from a required reading list to demonstrate the fact that they *have* done the reading and that they understand it. Summaries are also an important part of writing research papers: When you are writing about an area of knowledge, the first step is to read all the previously published works on the topic and summarize them early in your paper. In addition, students who participate in seminars often read different articles on a particular topic and summarize them for the rest of the group.

You've seen how important summaries are; now let's take a look at a summary and analyze the process of writing a summary. The following is based on the article by Isaac Asimov you read in Part One.

> According to Isaac Asimov, intelligence is a relative notion that is defined differently by different groups of people. In "What Is Intelligence, Anyway?" Asimov states that he has always done well on aptitude tests and that this is because the people who design such tests share his interests and training. If a mechanic or a carpenter or a farmer wrote an intelligence test, Asimov would do poorly. He explains that he is not good at work that he must do with his hands. Asimov claims, then, that intelligence is not absolute but determined by the society one lives in. In the world today, we gauge intelligence on the basis of intelligence tests designed by people in academia—not because such tests necessarily give us correct or absolute results, but because academicians have imposed these tests on us.

1. How long is the original article? How long is the summary?

   _____

2. What is the purpose of the first sentence of the summary? What information does it contain?

   _____

   _____

   _____

   _____

3. Look at the original article in Part One. How many main ideas are there? What are they? Now look at the summary. Are the same main ideas discussed? Are any missing?

_____

_____

_____

_____

_____

4. Notice the order of the ideas in the original. Is the same order used in the summary?

_____

5. Notice the use of details, facts, and illustrations in the original article. Do many of these details appear in the summary? Why or why not?

_____

_____

6. Whose ideas are expressed in the summary? How do you know? Do any opinions appear in the summary that are not in the original article? Why or why not?

_____

_____

_____

_____

7. Find examples of the language the writer of the summary uses to refer to Asimov's ideas; underline them. (The first one is <u>states that</u>.)

8. What verb tense is used in the original article? What tense is used in the summary?

_____

The summary you've just seen is an accurate, well-written one. Based on your answers to the preceding questions, what are some guidelines for writing a good summary? Write them below.

_____

_____

_____

_____

_____

_____

_____

_____

Citing Sources in Summaries

As you saw in the preceding example, certain words and expressions are used to cite, or refer to, the original author in a summary. (*Cite* means "to refer to.") Following is a list of the most common and useful of these expressions. Some of them are used in the preceding summary. Study them carefully. Each conveys a slightly different meaning. Discuss them with your teacher.

X (the original author)
{ states
claims
alleges
says
explains
writes
asserts
indicates
maintains }
that . . .

Practicing What You've Learned

In these exercises, you are going to be asked to write summaries of articles appearing in this book. For each one, keep in mind the guidelines for summary writing just outlined. In addition, make sure you use the expressions for citing the original author whenever it is appropriate. Each summary should be about one paragraph in length.

1. Summarize the article "Type A Behavior and Type B Solutions" in Chapter 4.

2. Write a summary of the newspaper article "An Off-the-Wall Success Story" about entrepreneur Porter Hurt in Chapter 5.

3. Write a summary of "Nonverbal Behavior: Some Intricate and Diverse Dimensions in Intercultural Communication," by Fathi Yousef, in Chapter 10.

4. Summarize the article "U.S. Passports Changing with Technology" in Chapter 11.

PART THREE

SYSTEMS FOR WRITING

INTRODUCTIONS AND CONCLUSIONS

In this chapter, you will see some simple and easy ways to write introductions and conclusions to your essays. As you progress in your study of English composition, you'll find that there are a variety of ways to introduce and conclude essays; you will see only a few of the basics in this section.

Introductions

An introduction is usually the first paragraph of an essay. Its purpose is to get the reader ready for the essay. The most important part of the introduction is the thesis statement, and as you've seen in previous chapters, the thesis usually appears at the *end* of the first paragraph of an essay and tells the reader what the essay will be about and how the discussion will be organized.

Any important task, such as reading an essay, requires adequate preparation. Therefore, the sentences in your first paragraph that precede the thesis serve to lead the reader into your most important idea. (*Introduce* means "to lead into.") Another purpose of the introduction is to capture the interest of a reader who may not otherwise be paying attention!

Three types of introductions will be discussed here: the general-to-specific, the anecdote, and the problem-solution types.

General-to-Specific This type of introduction consists simply of two to three sentences that lead to the thesis with decreasing levels of generality. In other words, the first sentence(s) of the introduction might be very general about the topic, the next sentence(s) slightly more specific, and the final sentence is the thesis itself. This kind of introduction looks like an upside-down triangle:

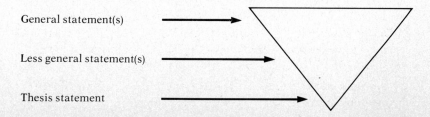

General statement(s)

Less general statement(s)

Thesis statement

Example:

At the present time, there is a great deal of interest in the use of computers in education. Public schools in the United States are acquiring computer equipment and programs. Many school districts have established computer resource centers and provide special training in the use of computers for teachers. The use of computers in education has important benefits for both students and teachers.

This is an introduction in the true sense of the word. The reader is led on a slightly narrowing path to the very specific thesis statement.

Anecdote An anecdote is a very short story. In an introduction, it is a short story told in three to five sentences, which is related to and leads the reader to the thesis statement. If it is well told, it makes the reader want to continue reading to see what happens next, or to see how this amusing, interesting, or shocking incident relates to the essay as a whole. This is the kind of introduction that "grabs" the reader.

Example:

As he climbed to the small room at the top of the stairs, he reached into his pocket to make sure the mandarins were still there. Once in the room, he set the mandarins on the desk in front of him. He glanced up at the bottle of kirsch on the shelf, pulled out his notebook, and prepared to write. As in the case of Ernest Hemingway, many writers need food and drink nearby to stimulate creativity.

Problem-Solution This kind of introduction is one that begins with a short (three-to-five sentence) explanation of a problem, one that the essay presumably will attempt to solve. The introduction ends with a thesis that presents the solution to the problem.

Example:

A recent study has shown that children watch an average of seven hours of television a day. This is of great concern to many parents. They worry that the violence on television will influence their children's behavior. They also worry that the frequent commercials for nonnutritive food will affect their children's eating habits. Parents are furthermore concerned that television programs present false information that could be detrimental. What can they do? The solution to this problem is simple: Parents should carefully select the programs their children watch and limit the number of viewing hours.

Notice that sometimes these types overlap. That is, an introduction might have the characteristics of more than one of the types described in this chapter.

Conclusions

You can think of a conclusion as just the opposite of an introduction, both in form and in function. Functionally, a conclusion prepares the reader for the end of your essay. It gives him or her a feeling of completion. A good conclusion makes the reader feel that you have said all you set out to say in your thesis, and gently leads him or her away from your work. In terms of form, the most common type of conclusion is just like the general-to-specific introduction, only upside down. In other words, it begins with a specific thought, a restatement of your thesis, moves on to a slightly more general statement about the topic, and ends with a very general thought on the topic as a whole. The key word is *restatement;* don't copy your thesis word for word. This will bore your reader. Additionally, if you've used the general-to-specific introduction technique, don't copy any of the other sentences word for word. The form and the ideas are the same, but the actual language in your conclusion should always be different from that in your introduction. You may think you don't have to please your reader anymore because you're at the end of your essay, but you do! You want him or her to be left with pleasant thoughts about you.

Study this example of a conclusion:

With all of these advantages for both teachers and students, it is easy to see why there is so much interest in the use of computers in education. Computers in business and in the home are also becoming commonplace. Before long, all people will have some contact with computers in their day-to-day lives.

Practicing What You've Learned

Exercise 1 Read the following essay introductions and state which type they exemplify: general-to-specific, anecdote, or problem-solution.

a. Five years ago, an old farm worker told me the story of his grandson, who is now a well-known optician in Managua. According to the old man, his boy had become spoiled by the capitalist society in which he lived. After he had finished his professional studies, he was more concerned about making money than filling the gap of optometrists in the rural area where he had been raised. It was during this conversation that I first realized that the majority of professionals in the health field tend to look at themselves as merchants who sell their products to the best bidder. As a result, we have a generation of health professionals who don't respond to the needs of the people. This must change, and in order to do this, we must change the established system and promote social responsibility among medical students as part of their training.

Type: _____

b. All students at our college have to pass English 1A and 1B before they can graduate. In other words, they must know how to write a good essay. Writing an essay is not an easy job, especially for most nonnative persons. It requires a great deal of time and practice. Even though writing an essay takes a lot of time and practice, it can be done in a less frightening way if you approach it step by step. The five steps in writing an essay are: finding a thesis, organizing ideas, writing a draft, revising the draft, and preparing the final copy.

Type: _____

c. Writing English well is not easy for anybody. Even some native speakers of English cannot write well. In particular, it is hard for nonnative speakers and especially for students in ESL classes. If people want to write well, not only do they need to know how to write, but they also need to know the process of writing. If you are an ESL student, you want someone to be able to read your essay easily and you want to improve your writing. You must know and follow three basic steps: thinking, writing, and revising.

Type: _____

Exercise 2 Rewrite the introductory paragraphs from three of your previous essays. Use each of the three introduction types described in this chapter.

Exercise 3 Rewrite the concluding paragraph of one of your previous essays. Use the specific-to-general type.

Assignments

1. Compare two different views on what intelligence is. Use the information you gathered in Part One. Cite authorities in your essay.

2. Discuss the effects of superior intelligence on an individual's daily life. Use the information you gathered in Part One. Try to incorporate the paragraph you wrote in Part One into your essay.

3. Summarize and react to Asimov's essay "What Is Intelligence, Anyway?" A summary-and-reaction essay looks like this:

   Paragraph 1: Summary of essay
                 Last sentence: your thesis (that is, your opinion on what the author has to say)

   Paragraph 2: Body

   Paragraph 3: Body

   Paragraph 4: Body (optional)

   Paragraph 5: Conclusion

   Note that, instead of an introduction, you lead up to your thesis with a summary of the article you are going to react to. Your thesis presents *your* point of view, either agreement or disagreement with the author, and your reasons for thinking the way you do.

4. Write a summary of and react to one of the articles you read when you did your research for Part One. Use the preceding organizational pattern.

5. What is the best measure of intelligence?

6. Agree with, disagree with, or explain the following quote: "There is no limit to either intelligence or ignorance."—Anonymous

PART FOUR

EVALUATING FOR REWRITING

Working with Your Partner

With a partner, make your own evaluation questionnaire for this chapter. Your evaluation should include questions that deal with all the important points you've learned about writing since you began this course. You may want to skim through each chapter. Make sure you include questions on the thesis statement, topic sentences, paragraph development and organization, and introductions and conclusions. Write your questions in the following space. You can also devise your own system to rate each other's papers.

1. _____
   _____

2. _____
   _____

3. _____
   _____

4. _____
   _____

5. _____
   _____

6. _____
   _____

7. _____
   _____

8. _____
   _____

9. _____
   _____

10. _____
    _____

Etc. _____
     _____

Working on Your Own

Using the questionnaire, answer the questions about your own paper. Consider these answers and your partner's comments before you rewrite your essay.